AF394464

NEO RAUCH
PROPAGANDA

David Zwirner Books

Tara, 2018

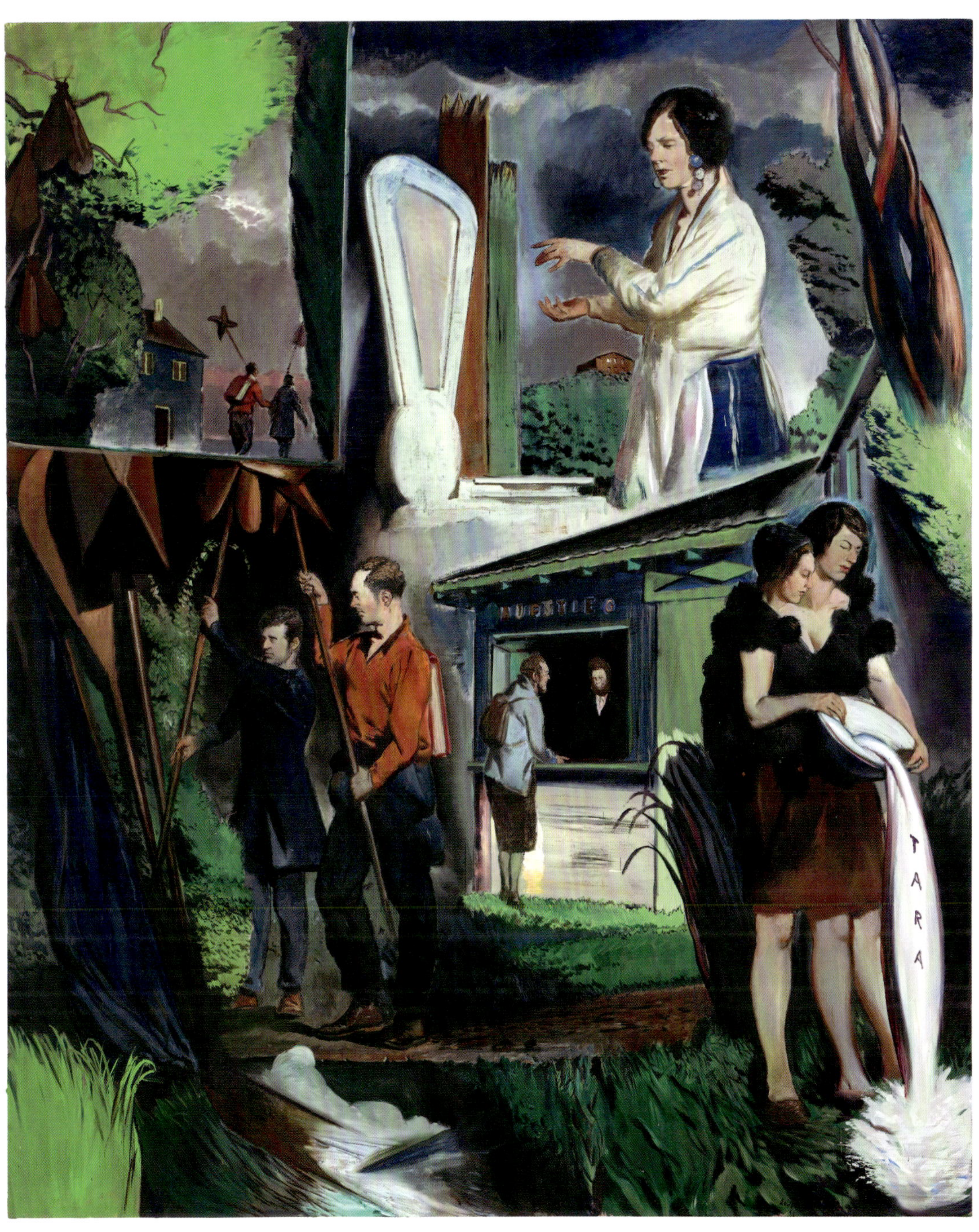

TARA

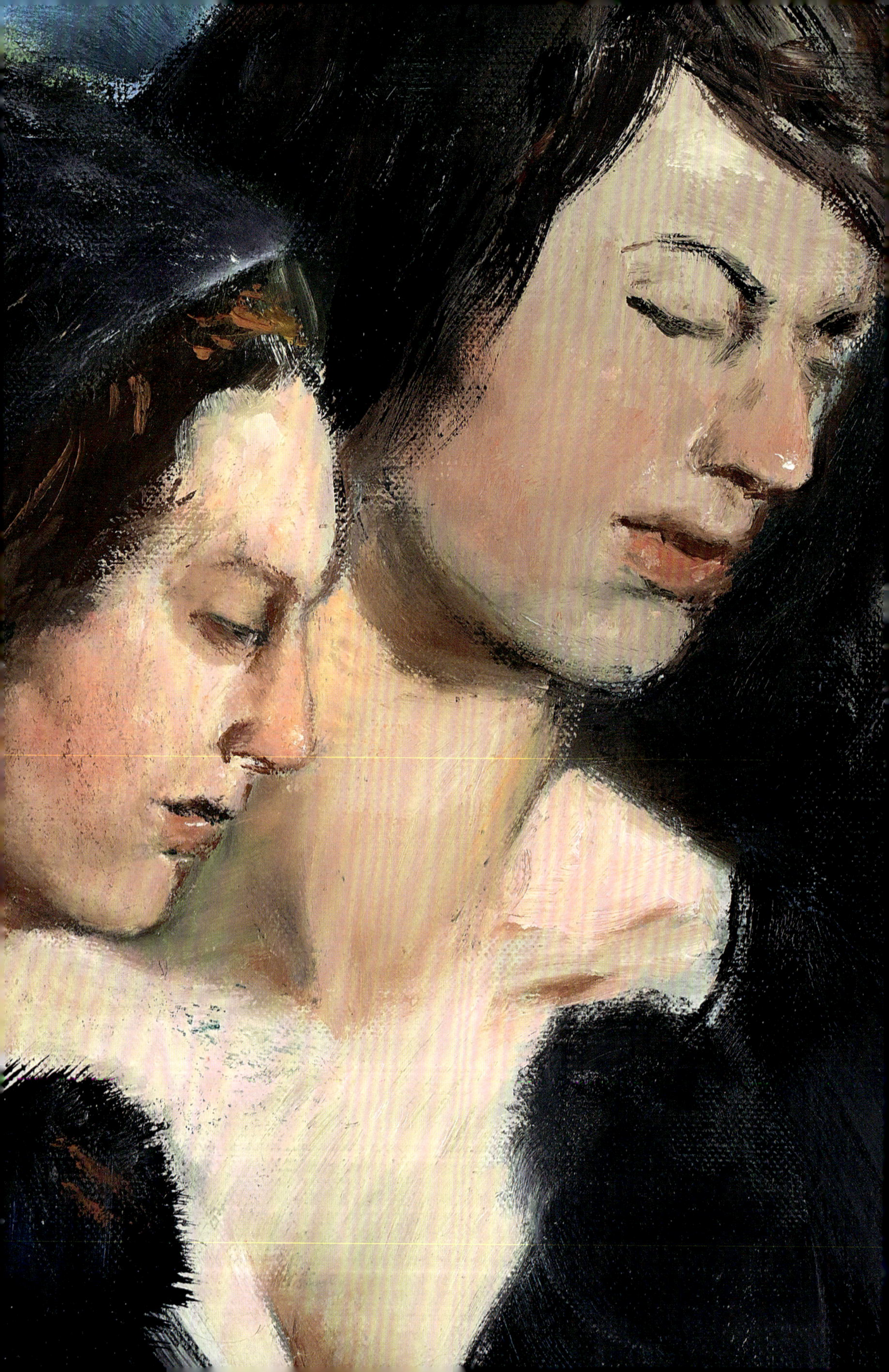

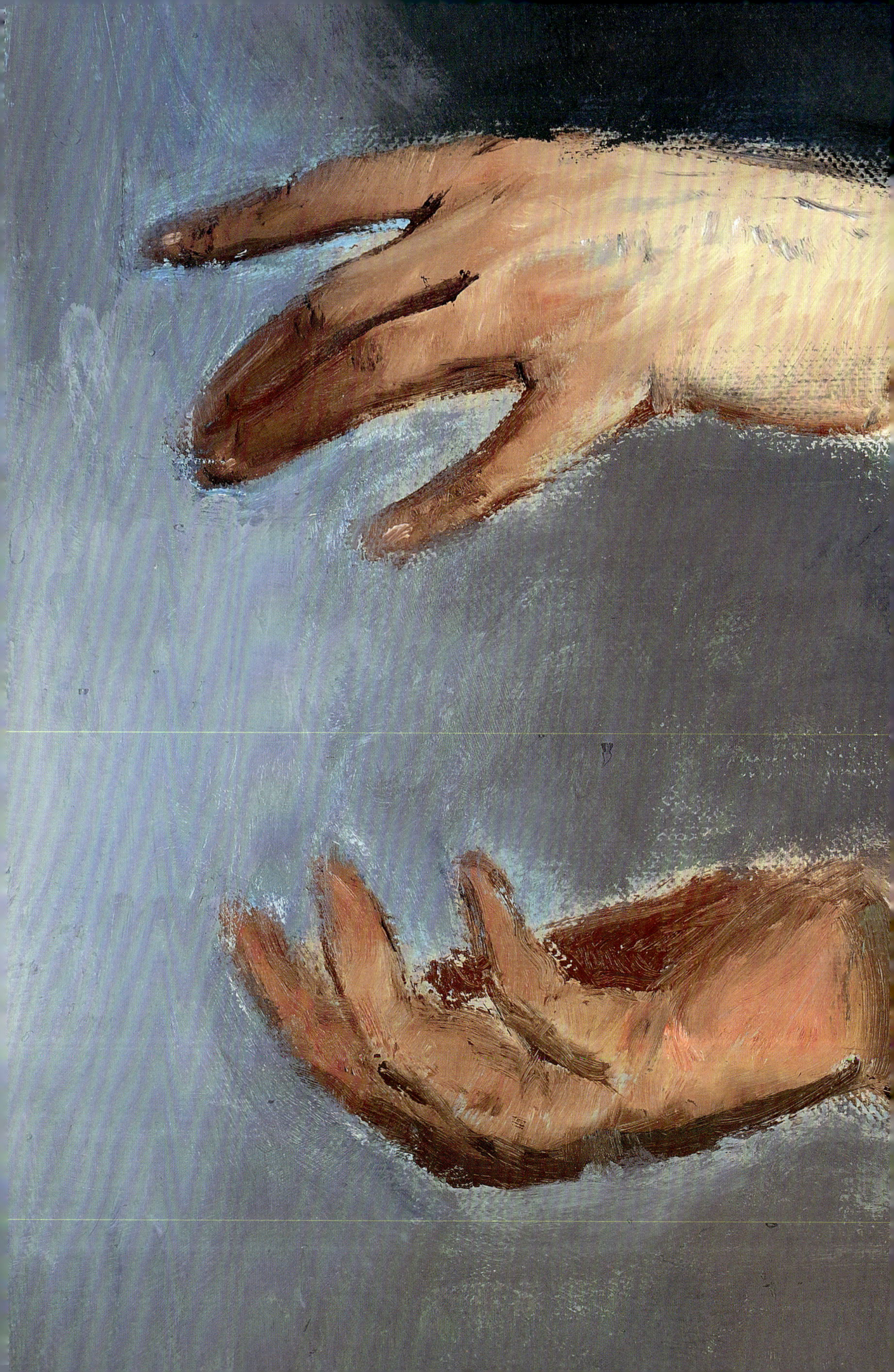

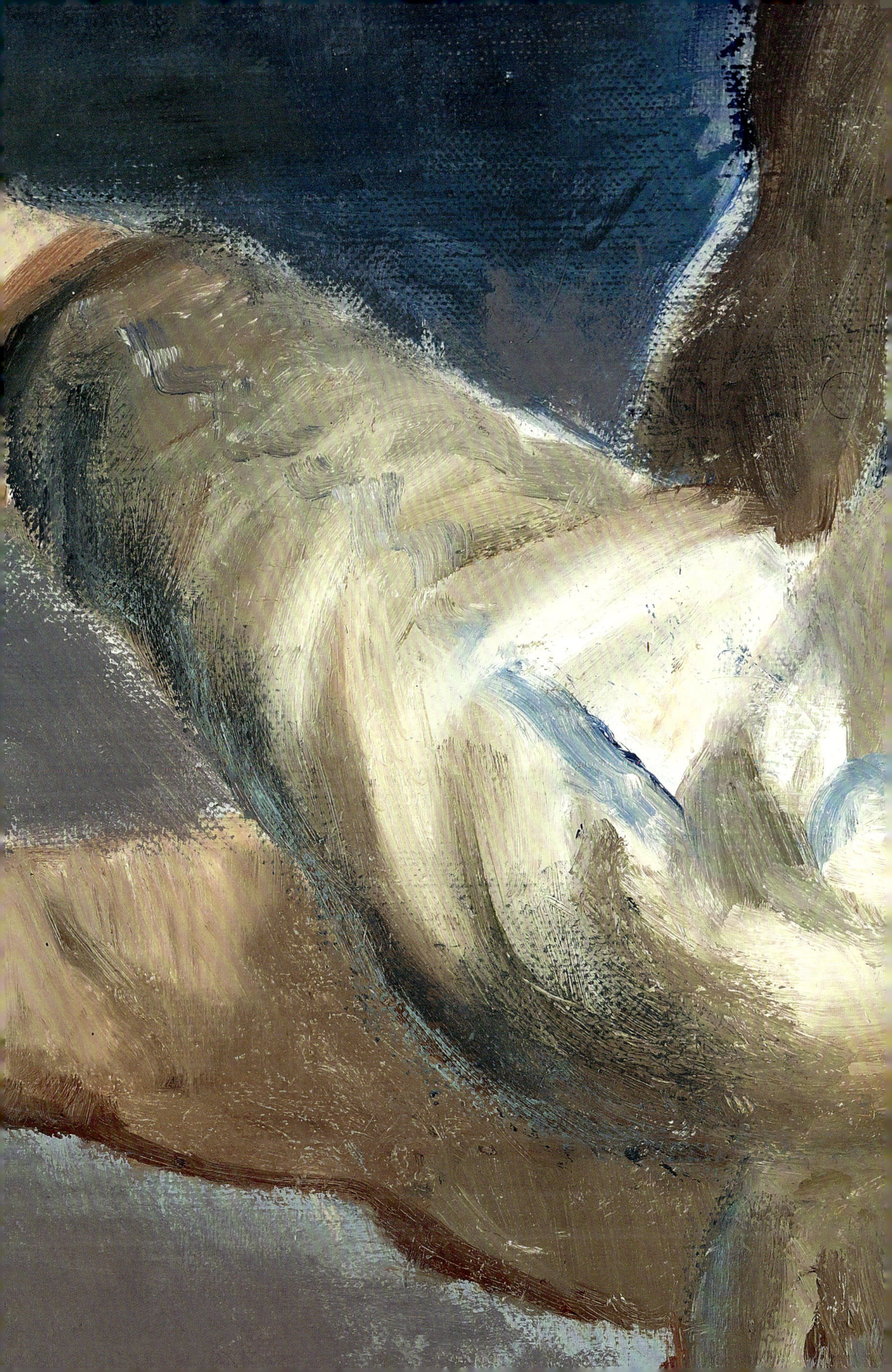

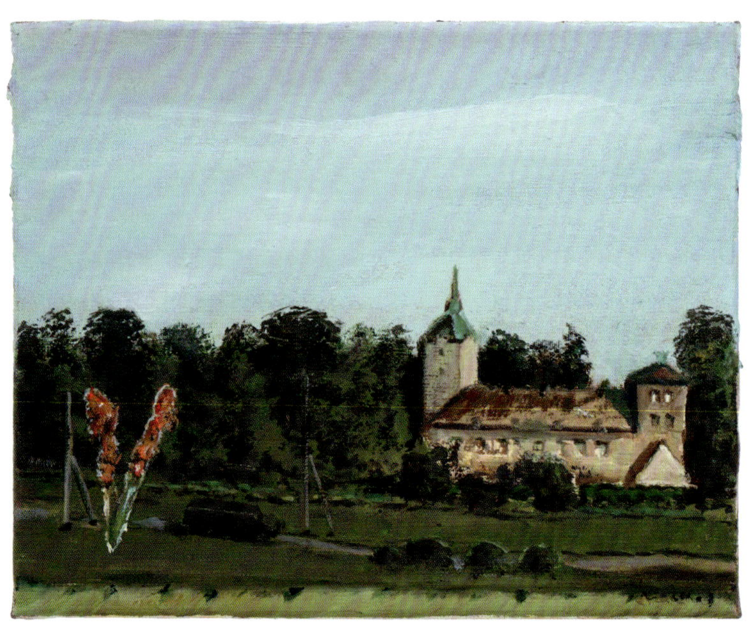

Zahler, 2018

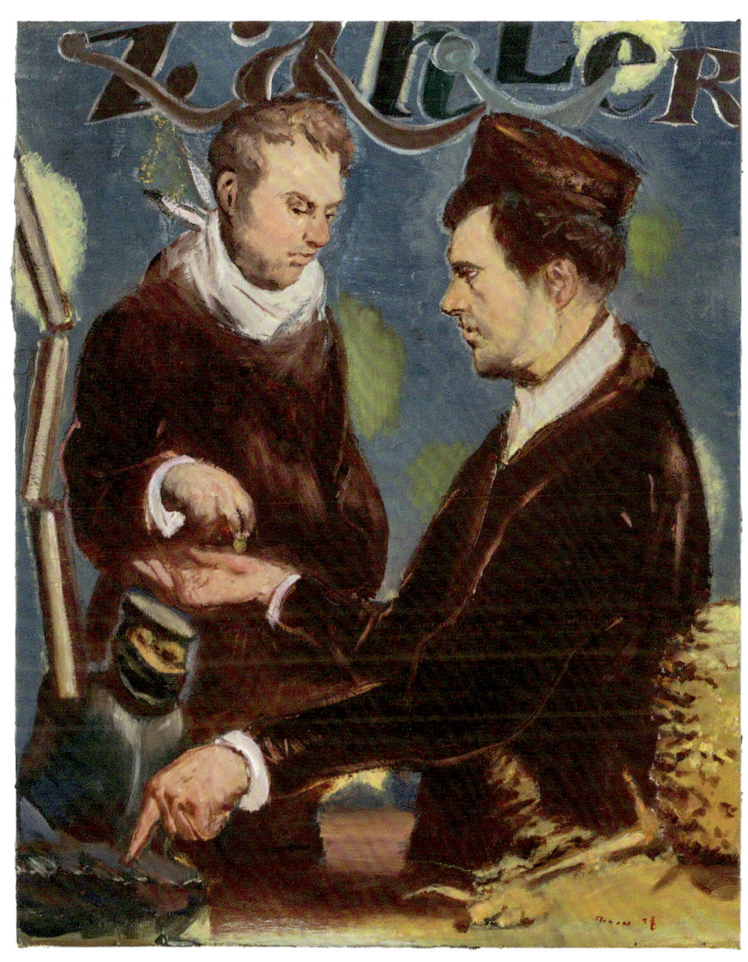
ZILLER

Кар, 2018

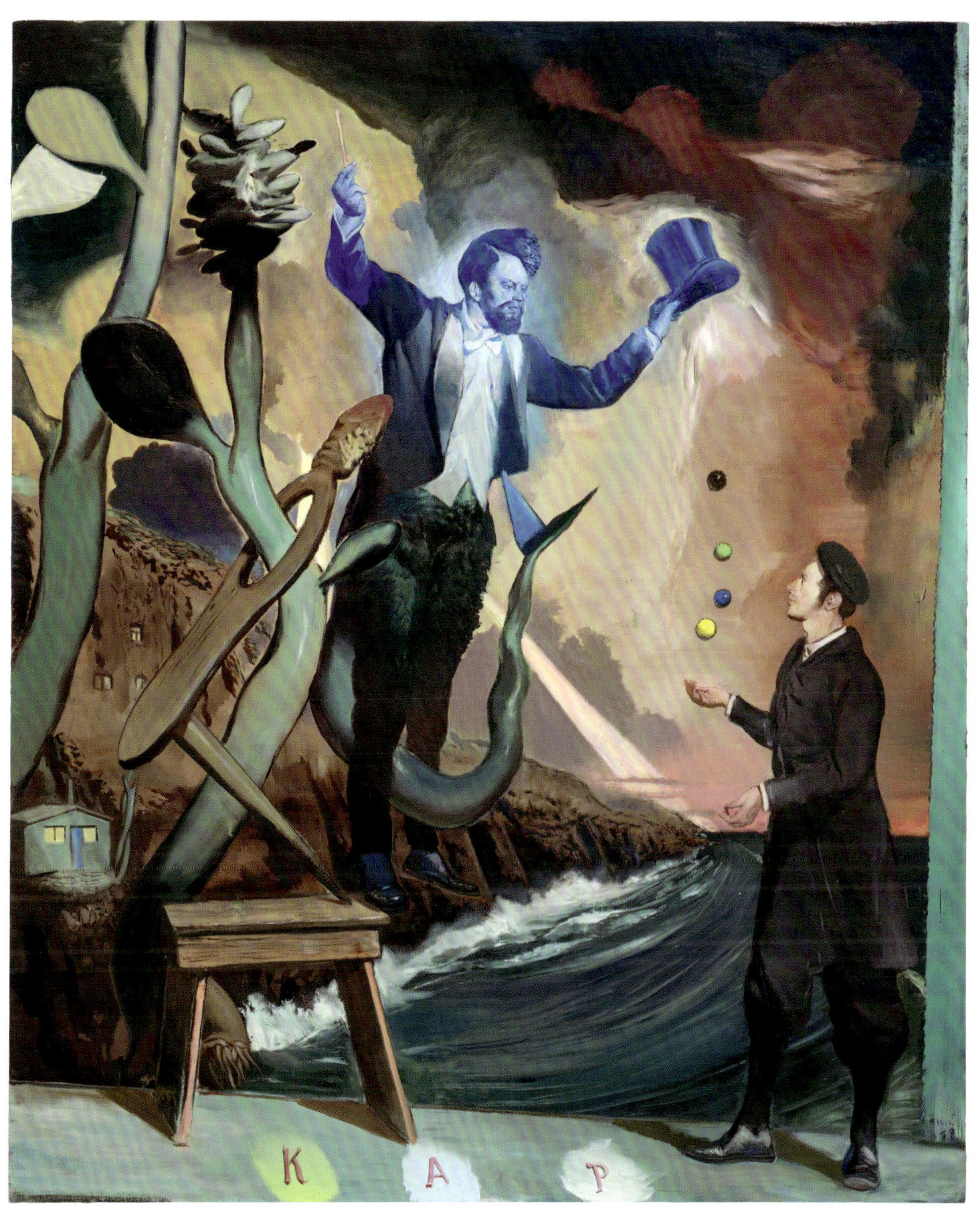

К А Р

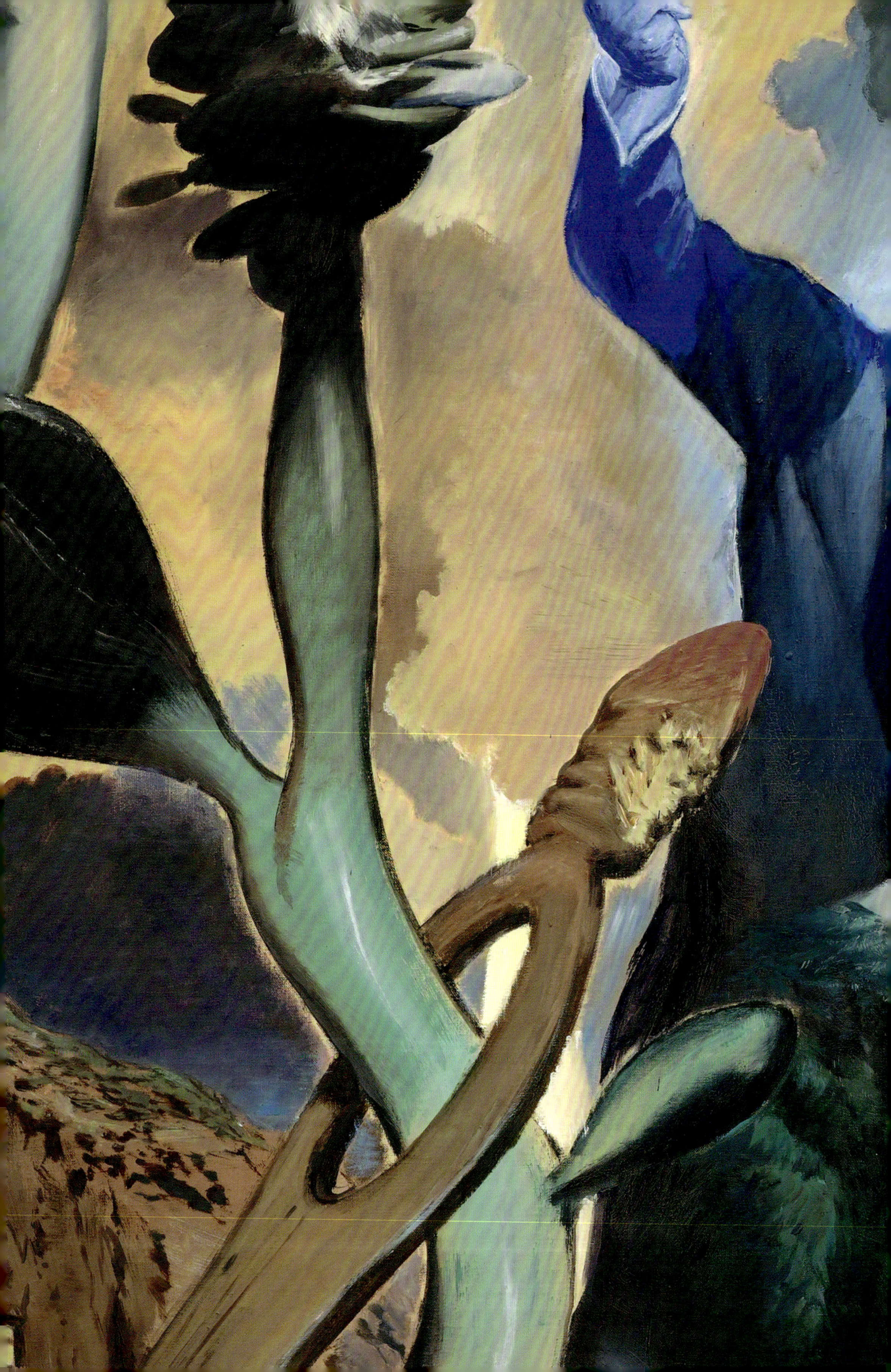

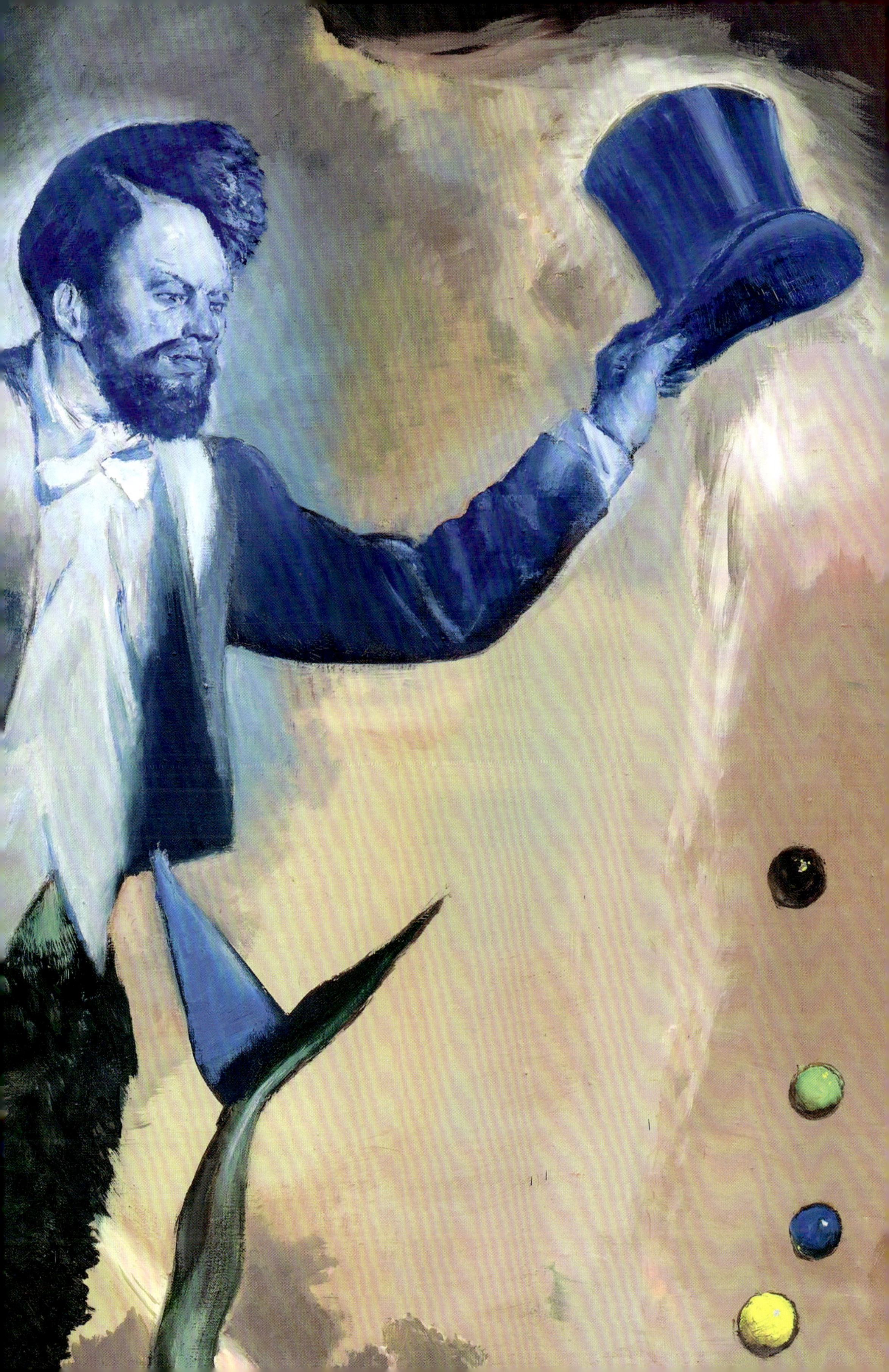

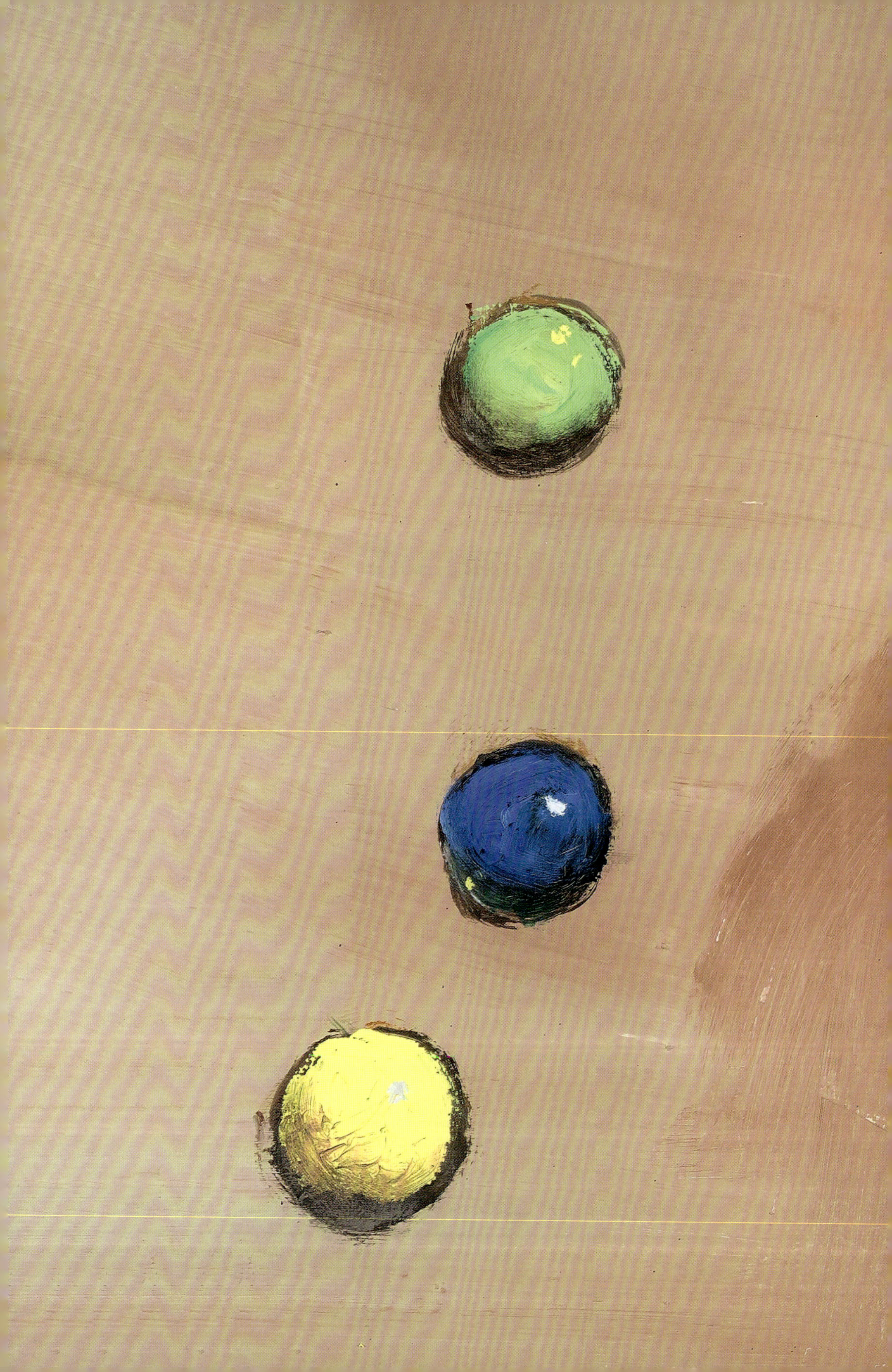

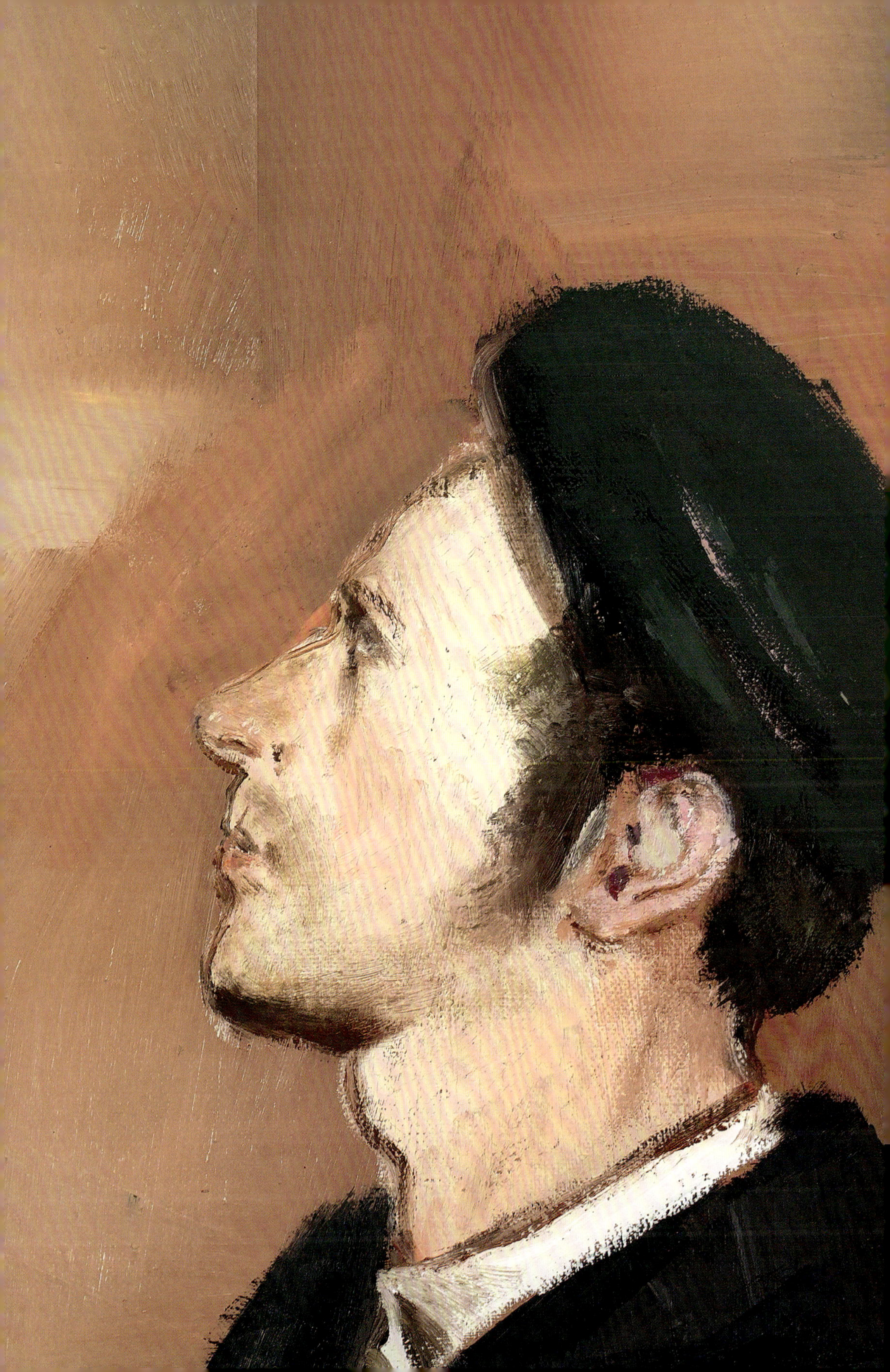

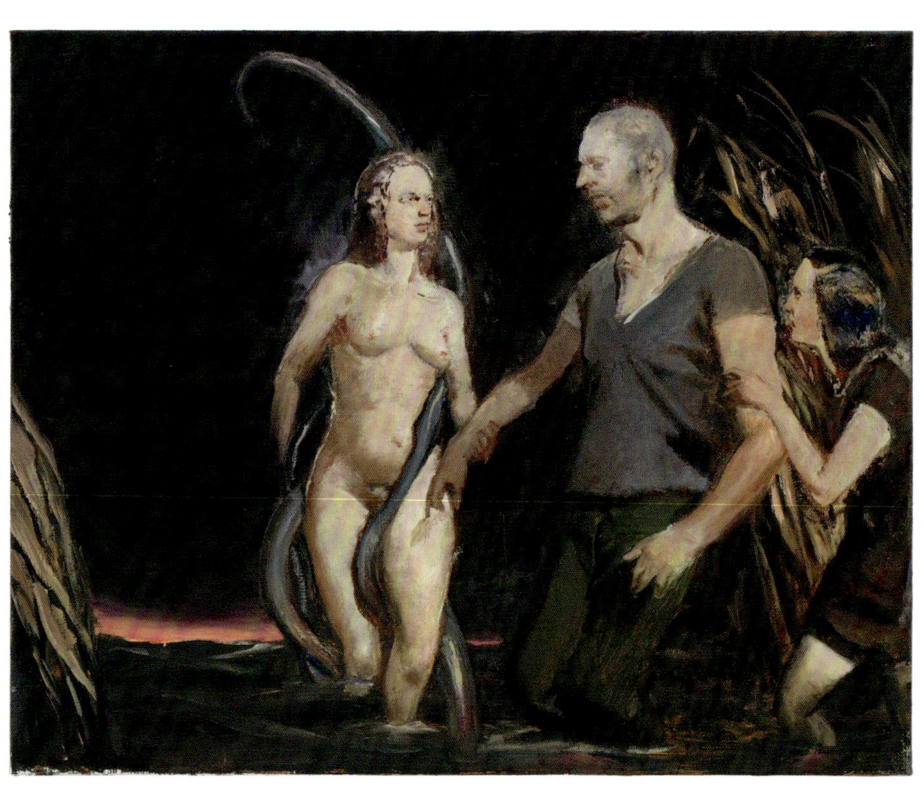

Der Wächter, 2018

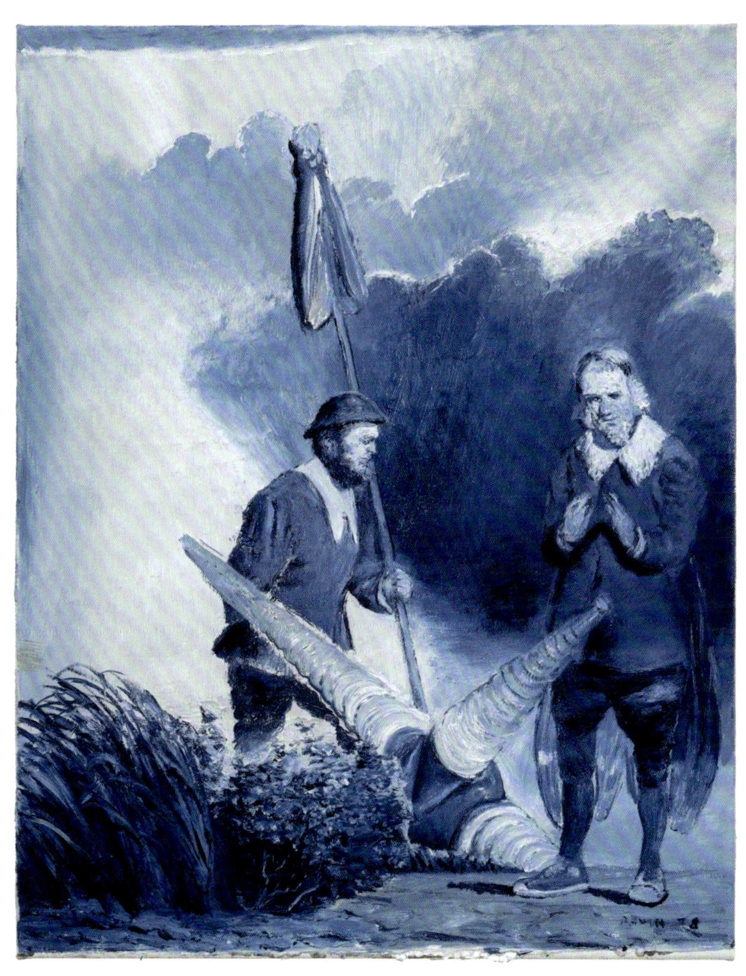

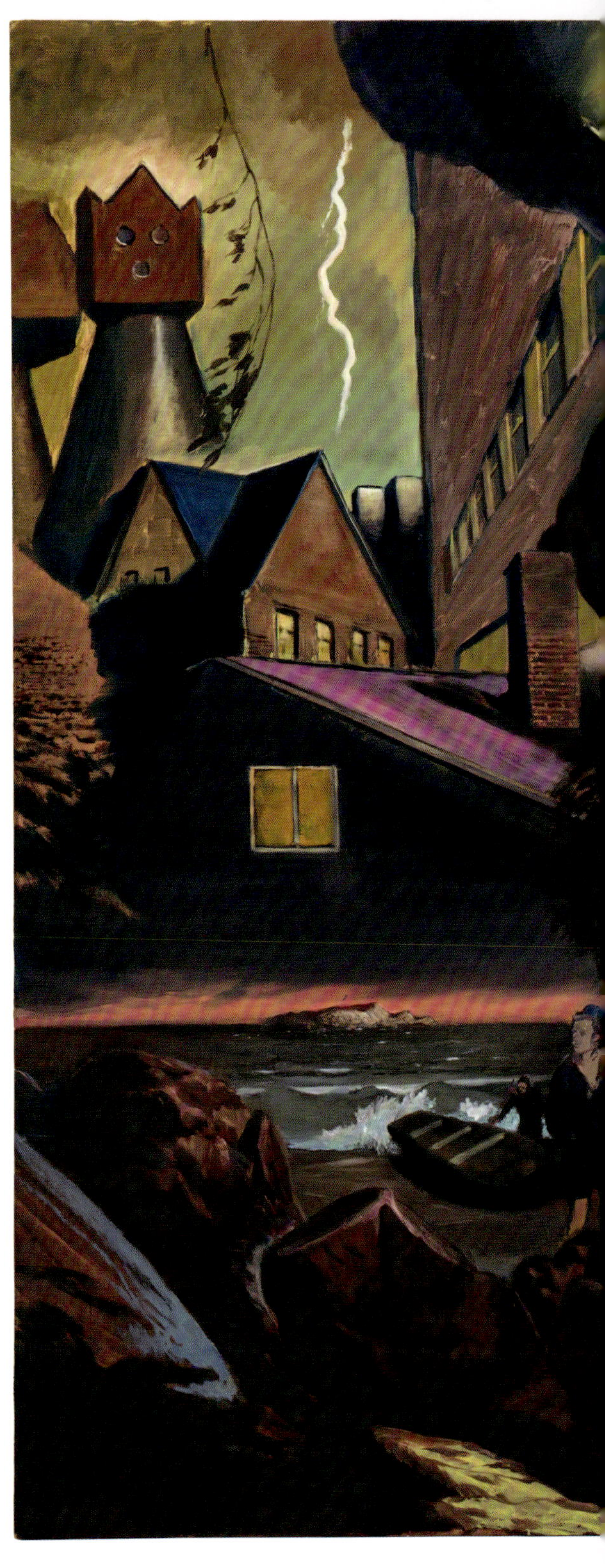

Die Herrin, 2018

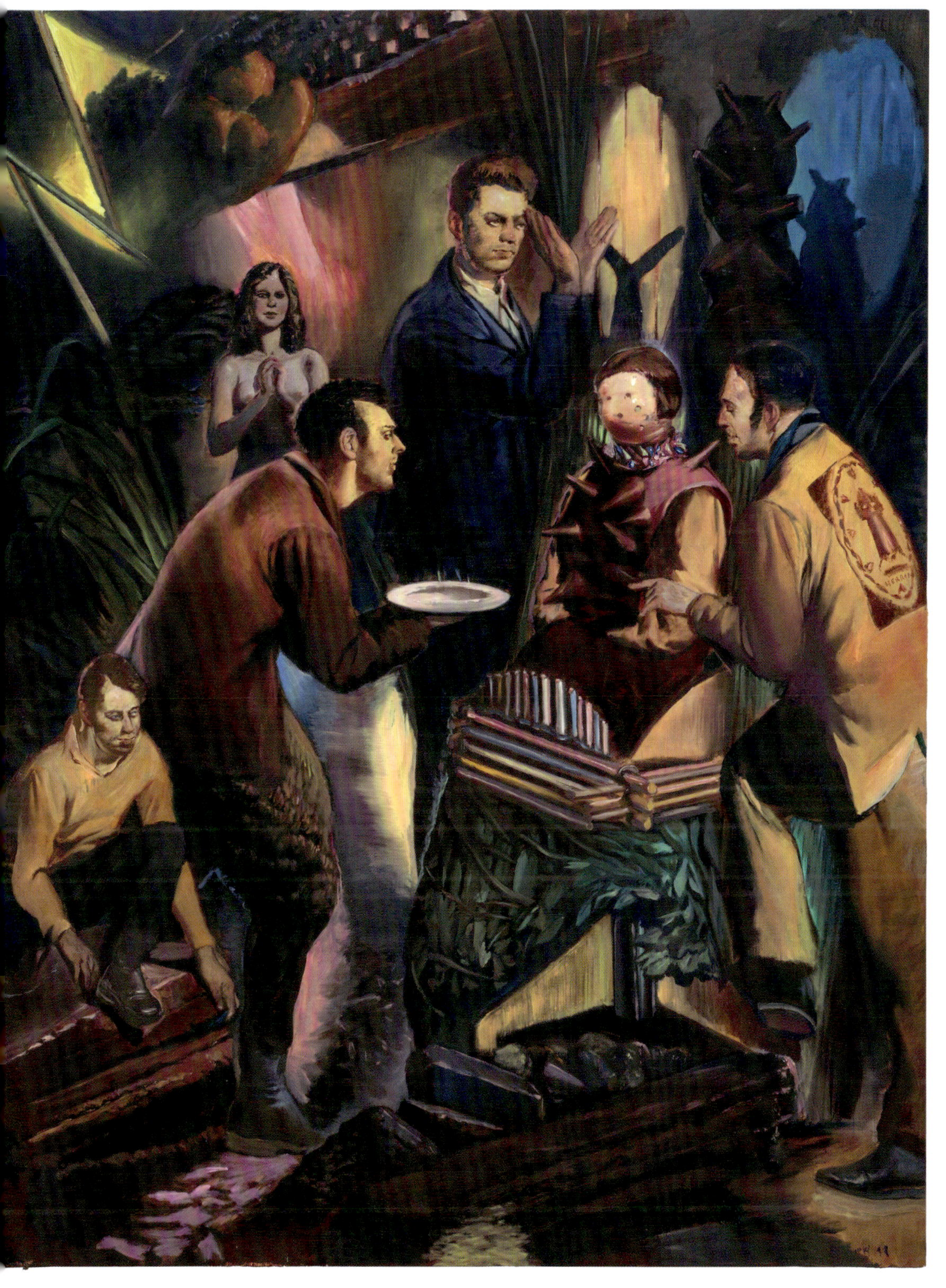

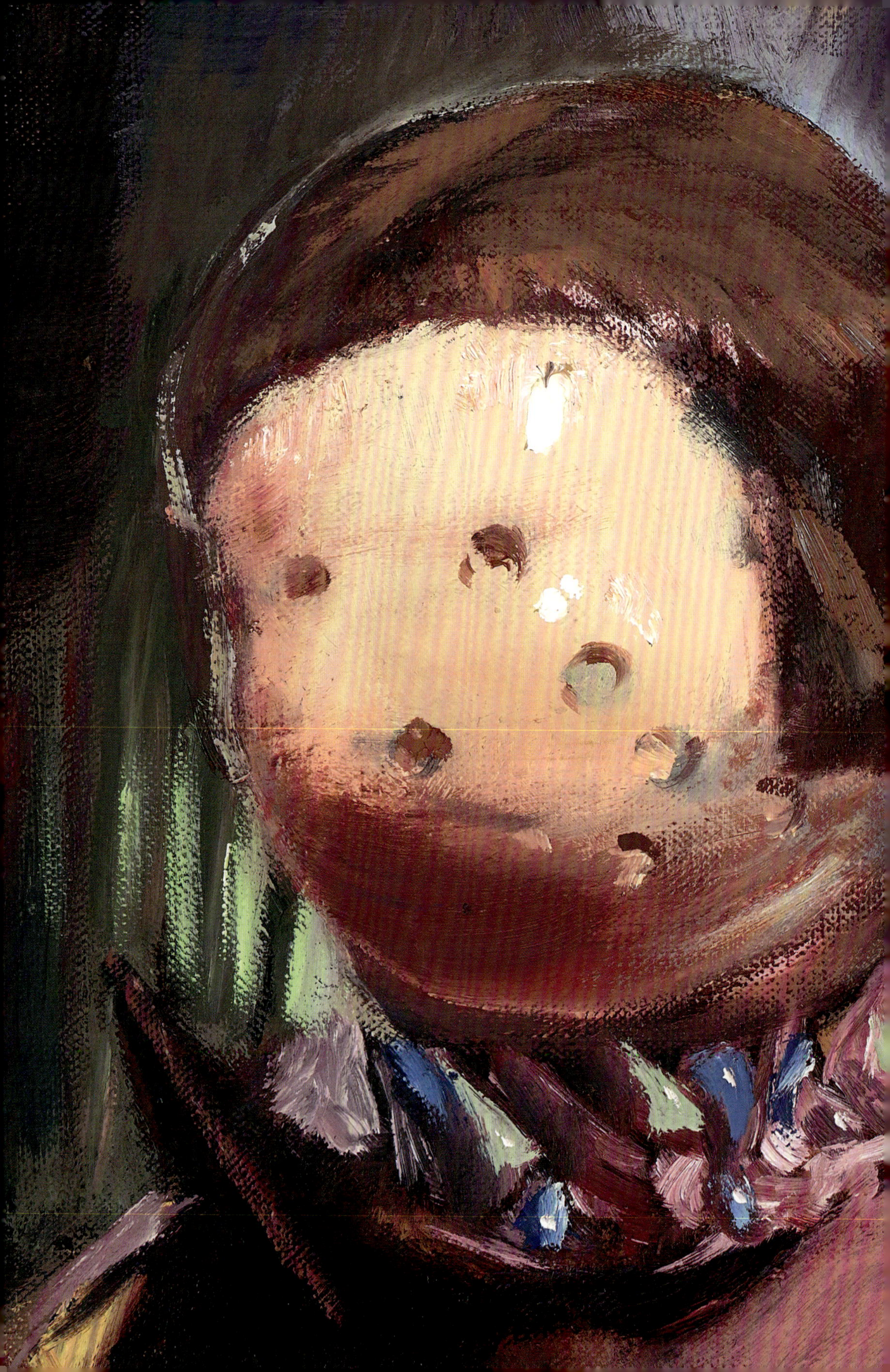

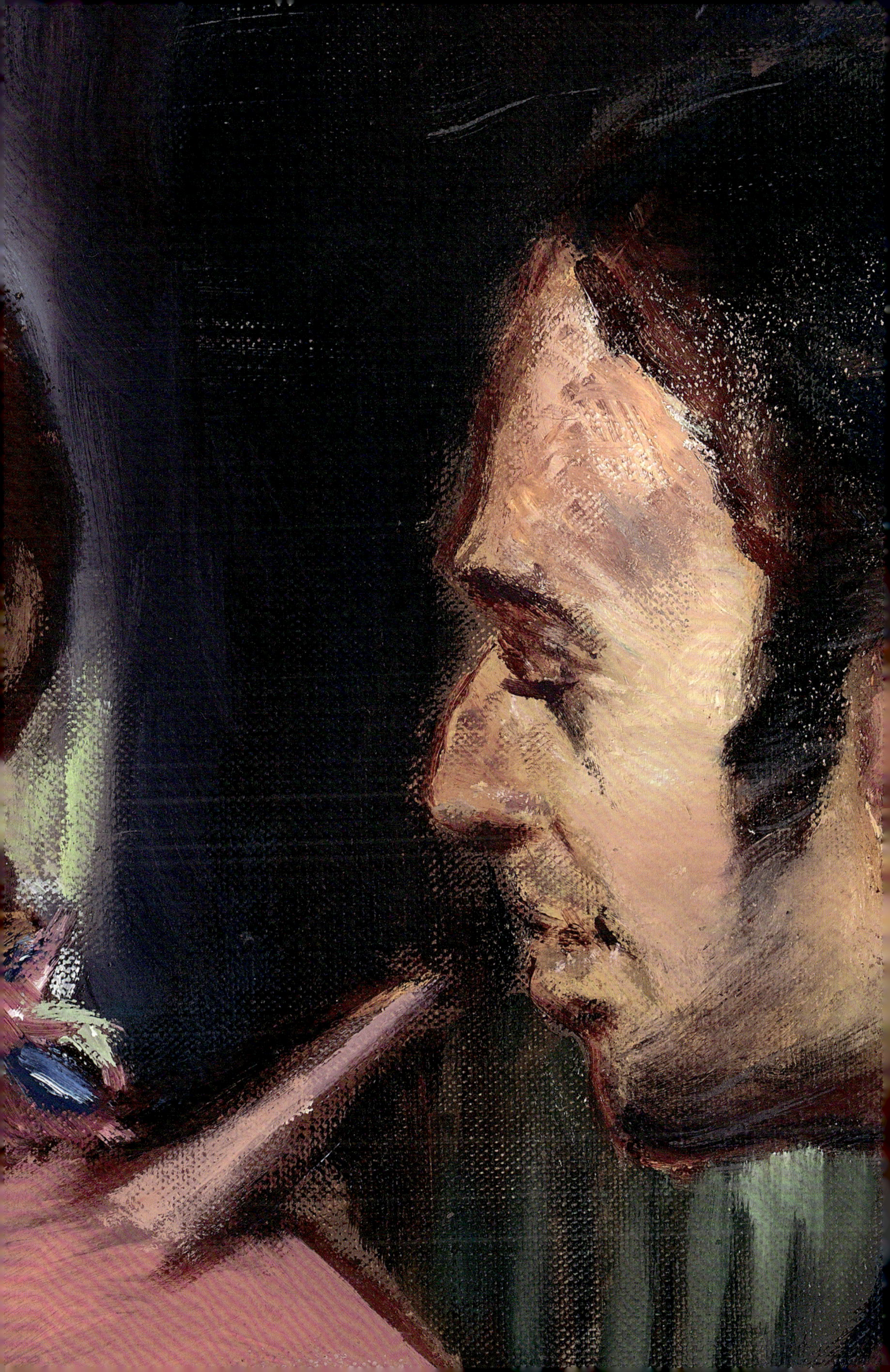

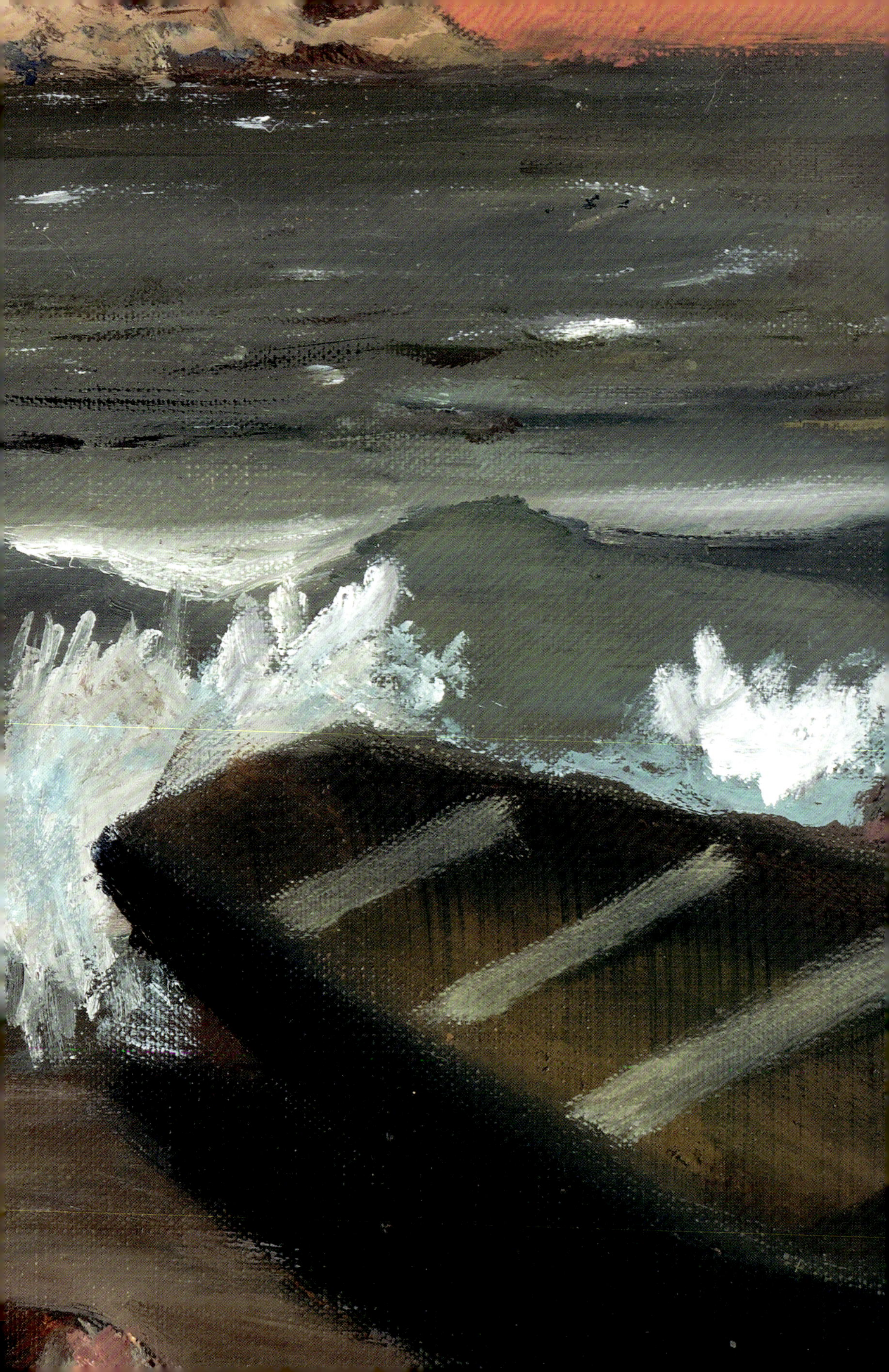

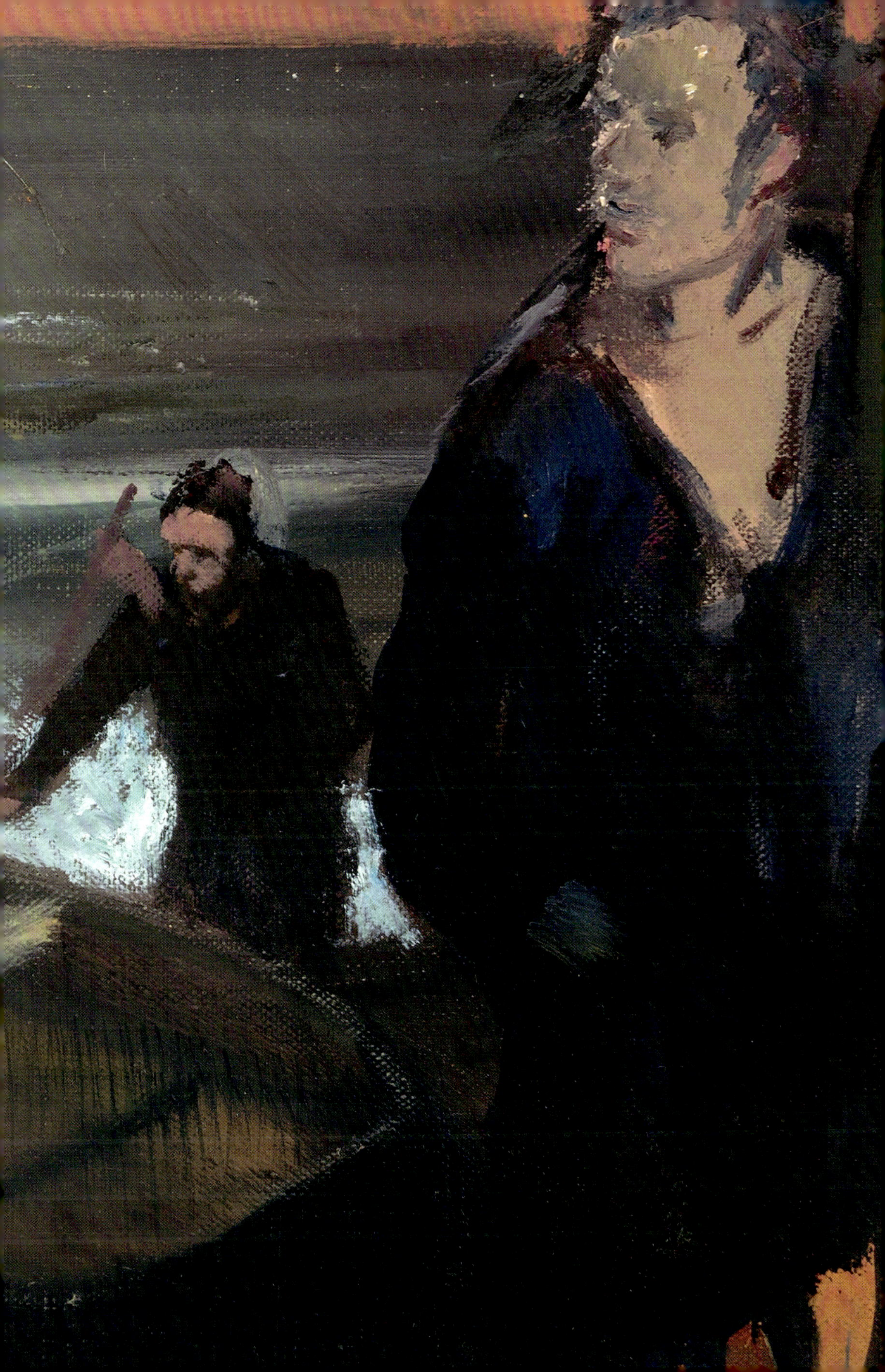

Becoming Caligari
A Fantasy Inspired by Neo Rauch's Art
Daniel Kehlmann

I

Once upon a time, there was a master. He was no longer young but not yet old, and word of him had reached every corner of the earth. He spent his life far from the cities, and from the royal courts, too, he kept his distance, for he wanted neither to bend the knee nor to associate himself with the trite chatter of the crowd. Thus he lived in a hut in the forest. The bees gave him honey, the stream clear water, and he knew where berries and edible mushrooms were to be found.

From time to time, people came. Each journeyed long, some with walking sticks, others on horseback, one even on an old bicycle. When they found him, they were relieved and could hardly believe that he stood before them in the flesh, for some had begun to suspect on the way that he was merely a legend.

When he was a child, a witch lived in the forest. Even then, she was quite weary, shrunken with age, wrinkled as leather, and sad, too, because she had seen so much live and grow and pass away. Long since unable to ride her broom, she had switched over to a rusty tractor, but she still had a few potent mushrooms and herbs, and she knew where to find the dwellings of the Little People, whom one could see only if one knew the right words of the ancient language. The master himself had never seen the Little People, but he still remembered the day when the witch, accompanied by a somewhat feral unicorn, sighing and muttering and almost certainly drunk, left the forest forever.

Sometimes he told the visitors to his hut of this sight. "A master is not a teacher," he said to them. "I cannot teach you anything. I can only say what I have seen."

They would sit at his feet like children. A knight who had come from the north leaned his sword against the trunk of the old oak, and a hangman from Nuremberg who had spent many years searching for the master even quit texting on his phone. A young woman, spellbound, adjusted her glasses; a journalist at first went on taking notes, but then stopped, because what he was hearing was too important. And when the master fell silent, which he did more and more often, they heard the bees buzzing; they heard the rustling and whispering and murmuring of the wind in the leaves. And only

now and then did they hear the noise of an airplane making
its way between the clouds overhead, concealed by the crowns
of the trees.

II

Recently, I had a confused dream. When I awoke, I thought
of Germany. It was not what had disturbed my sleep, but now
I could think of nothing else. And when I got up and looked
out the lightly misted window into the early New York morning,
I thought for probably the thousandth time of the Neckarauen,
the meadows by the Neckar River. "Then Germany would be
like the word *Neckarauen*," a great writer once wrote. And I also
thought of the work of a Leipzig painter, of his somber figures,
often clad in old clothing and locked inside themselves, not
infrequently surrounded by forest green or standing beside
dilapidated houses almost certainly not their own. I thought
of the strangely vague threat hanging over these painted
people, and I thought of Protestantism, which long ago set
out from Germany on its way into the world, and which teaches
that every human being is, in the end, alone with himself and
with God—a worldview that never could have come from
the South. *What is German?* I thought. And I thought: *What a
senseless question!* And I thought: *But it must be asked.*
And I thought: *It's early, go back to bed! Maybe you'll find it
again, your dream from before.*

III

Once upon a time, there was a knight. He ventured forth on a
quest—as knights have done from time immemorial—but didn't
know what he was seeking. On the hood of his old VW hovered
a reflection of the sun, and this, he decided, would be the star
that he would follow. On the back seat lay his sword, on the
passenger seat his plumed helmet. He used to have a flag,
but he had lost it somewhere. It had been embroidered with a
coat of arms, which had given him great pleasure.

He searched and searched. In his youth he had known a true
master, who lived alone with his bees. The master's words had
moved him to the depths of his soul, and even if he had long
since forgotten them, he still felt this deep inner stirring as if
he had heard them only yesterday.

There was also a woman who was precious to him. He
had sworn eternal love to her, in the old courtly manner, and

since then each victory had been an homage rendered to her, and in the evening he wrote her songs. And the fact that she didn't answer his messages and had gotten married years ago and now lived with her husband and two children in Düsseldorf in no way diminished his devotion.

Thus he journeyed through the land, having many an adventure and surviving countless perils, and his faithful sword was nicked in battle.

IV

I often think about the men to whom we owe the cathedrals. They were the greatest artists of their era, and their works outlast the centuries, but we don't know their names. It would have been a simple matter to leave them to us; they only would have had to chisel them into stone. But to sign their works wouldn't even have occurred to them. They saw themselves as craftsmen. They were masters.

And usually, they didn't finish. The Cologne Cathedral took six hundred years; only in the romantic nineteenth century was it completed—and distorted by this very completion. For its true form is the unfinished one, as seen in old paintings: the half-built tower, the empty space next to it, the skeleton of Gothic supports, which do not even have to bear the heaviness of a roof. This indeed is what it looks like, the face of the German Middle Ages.

V

Near a city that has no name, or none worth mentioning, the knight undertook his greatest adventure. His adversary was terrible. Some called him an evil sorcerer, others a dragon. Some heard the knight had battled a thinking machine, while others submitted that this by itself was not saying anything— since all of them, man, dragon, sorcerer, were nothing but thinking machines, after all—and still others claimed it had been the mysterious Caligari. But whoever or whatever it was, the knight finally faced his destiny in the form of this adversary. It was the hardest of all tests, the greatest battle.

When it was over, he didn't know whether he had won or lost. How could he tell? How could he be sure when there was no referee there to decide?

His sword, in any case, had been left on the battlefield, and he could no longer find the VW either. The world seemed changed in some unaccountable way. The color had drained from things as if there were a leak somewhere, and worst of all, every word suddenly seemed to refer only to itself and no longer to any object out there. When he said "shoe" or "table" or "bread" or "shirt," only the sounds his mouth made remained, while the solid things that they once indicated had nothing more to do with them. He felt as if something dark were moving through the world—a heaviness and a great exhaustion.

But I haven't even lived that long, he thought. *Am I already getting old?* And he wondered whether there might actually be a grail somewhere that bestowed eternal life on the one who drank from it. It didn't seem very likely—and even if it did exist, how was he going to find it in his condition?

He began to suspect that he was perhaps nothing but a figure in a painting, where things might seem to make sense, but only at first glance, only for a moment, while in truth they become more and more enigmatic the longer one looks. *Others can view the painting*, he thought. *They can take a step back, gain distance, recognize how it all coheres. But I, being in it myself, cannot do so. I will never see the whole. I will never understand.*

VI

After I got up, simply unable to fall back asleep after thinking about Germany, I walked across Washington Square, past benches with students reading and street musicians and peddlers of "Impeach Trump" buttons and the many squirrels that, in apparent cheerfulness but actually in fear because they sensed winter approaching, scrambled for the nuts retirees threw to them.

And suddenly, Doctor Faust came to my mind. Not Goethe's classical Faust, but the old Doctor Johann Faust of folk legend, who was born in Knittlingen and died nowhere. I have no doubt that he existed. And if he did, I thought, as I stopped next to a pianist (really, here in the park, in front of the stone arch of Washington Square, someone had set up a grand piano and was playing Bach, and this was probably not a dream), then that old bargainer with the devil could still be alive today. Over there, on the other side of the Atlantic, he could be in his hometown of Leipzig, drinking in Auerbach's Cellar, I thought, or even here, in downtown Manhattan—why not? What might his face look like, after so many centuries? A painter who could depict that, I thought, would be a great painter.

A few paces farther on, I bought a coffee, and while I waited for the grumpy vendor at his coffee stand to fill the paper cup, it seemed as if I saw, beyond the playground with its accident-proof equipment, a knight. He looked lonely and somewhat despondent. He actually looked like everyone else; he was wearing neither armor nor weapons, and I could not even say what marked him as a knight, but there was no doubt. For a moment, I considered speaking to him. But what was I supposed to say? I couldn't help him.

And I thought of the Leipzig painter whose work speaks of all this—old German figures, the feeling that confused dreams are reality and reality a confused dream, the great threat and the small worry and the knowledge that the whole has no meaning and that in this very knowledge lies one meaning of art. And as I followed the knight with my eyes, everything seemed transformed. Even Washington Square, with its students and street musicians, appeared to me like a version of the old, dark Germany, with its unfinished cathedrals and its bizarre sepia silent films. "I know not who I am," goes a saying from the baroque period, the provenance of which is a matter of dispute. "I know not whence I come. I know not whither I go. It's a wonder I'm in such good cheer."

A godless saying, such was Martin Luther's verdict. Because, for the true Christian, it's just the opposite: he knows whence and whither. And the astonishing thing: he is nonetheless sad.

VII

"You must become Caligari!" says the most brilliant silent film of all, which casts its protagonist into a gothic labyrinth of delusion. The film takes place in a world warped by a deranged imagination, full of gothic columns and angles and half-timbered houses and medieval structures without sense, but in truth, as it turns out, it takes place entirely inside what was then called a lunatic asylum. The protagonist's breakdown manifests itself in his seeing the words "You must become Caligari!" written wherever he looks.

And it is never explained what it actually means to "become Caligari," and for that very reason you can never get it out of your head. Is it a threat or a promise? Whatever it may be, it seems to be a fate. Perhaps each of us must sooner or later become Caligari.

VIII

I walked out of the park and left them all behind me: the homeless knight and Doctor Faust and the milling students and the rhythmic noise of the street musicians and the squirrels. And Caligari, whoever that is. And I also stopped thinking about Germany. As I crossed the street, I imagined I was in a forest and could hear the stream murmuring. And I imagined the bees buzzing and giving me honey. The world seemed vast, dark, and confusing, and I also knew, of course, that in reality the bees are dying out, but against this I was, as against so much, powerless.

And it was a wonder I was in such good cheer.

Translated from the German by Ross Benjamin

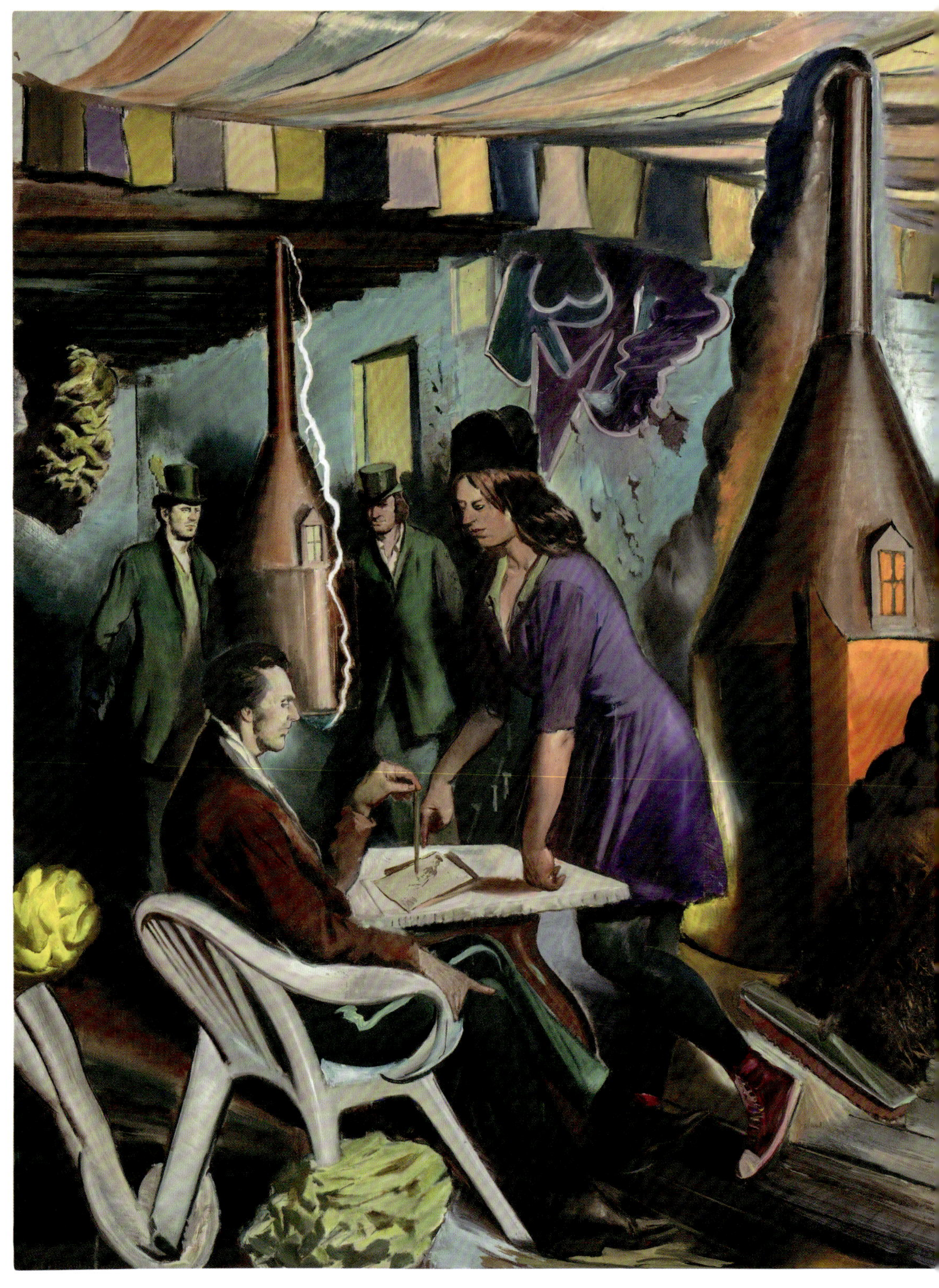

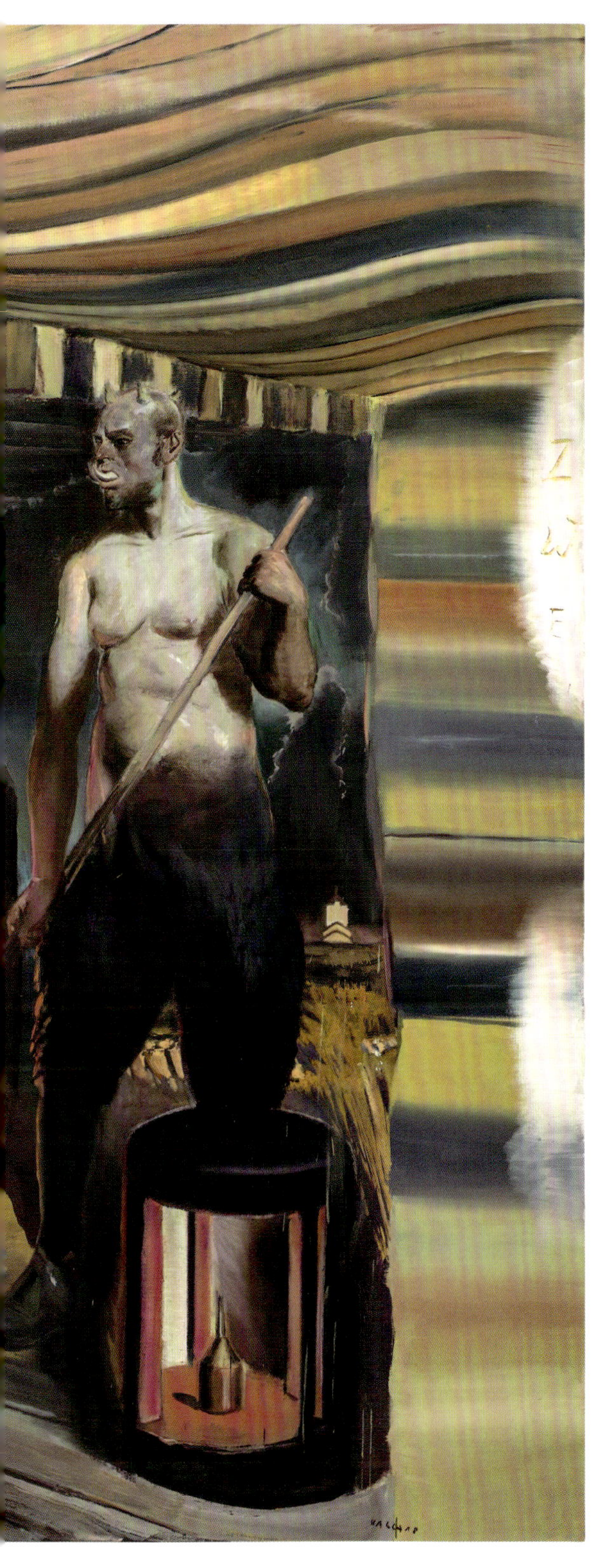

Zweifel, 2018

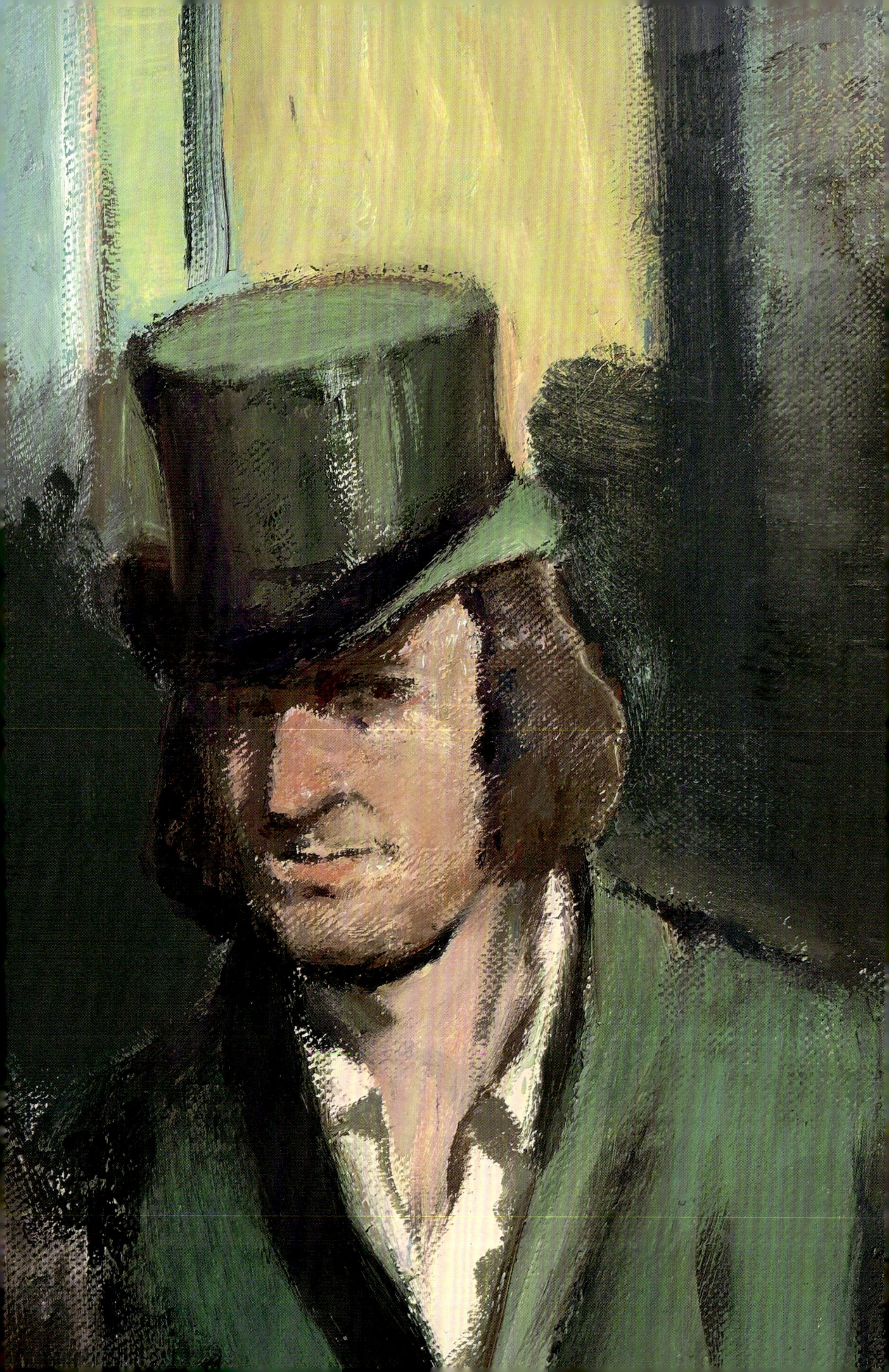

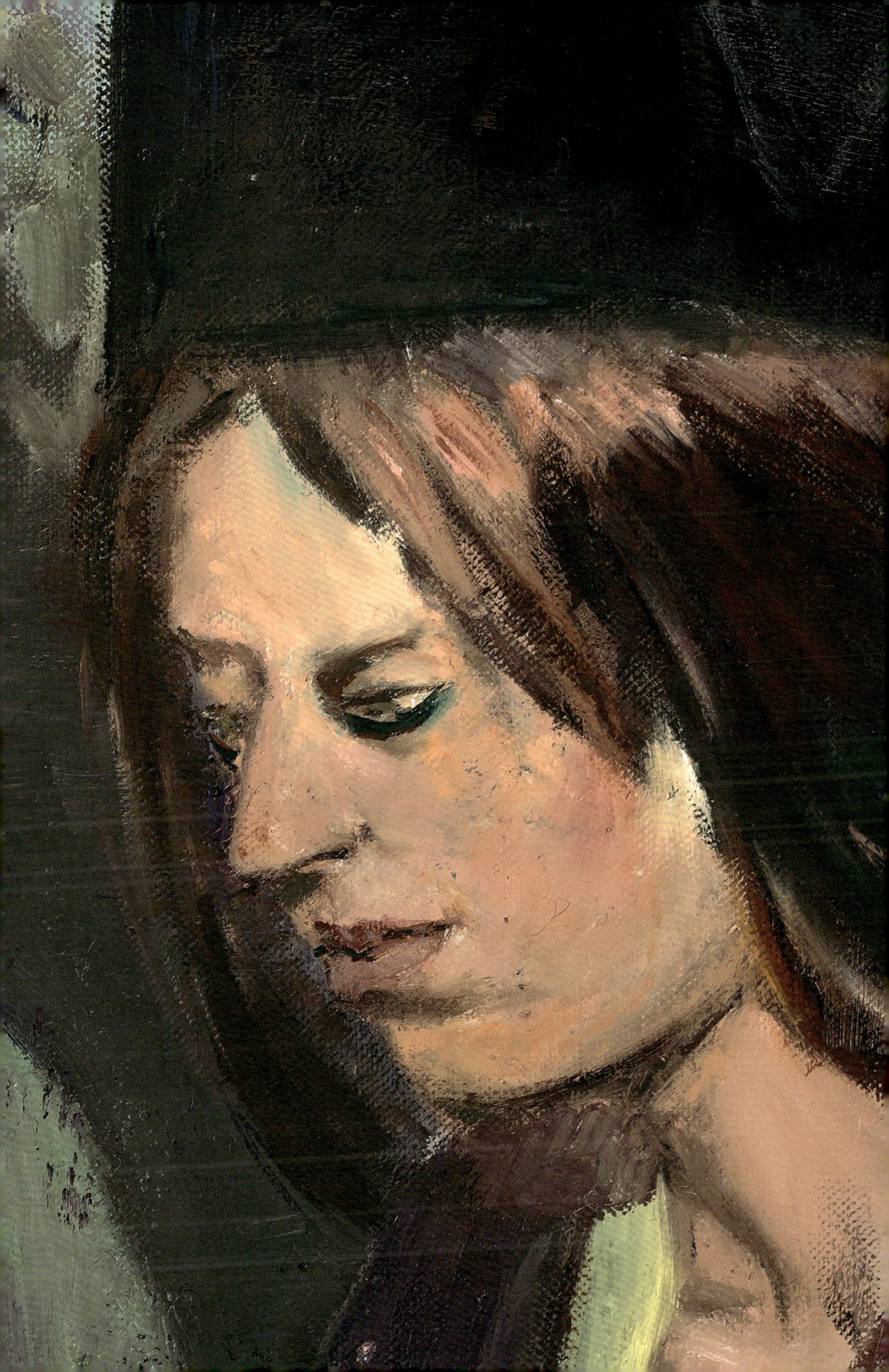

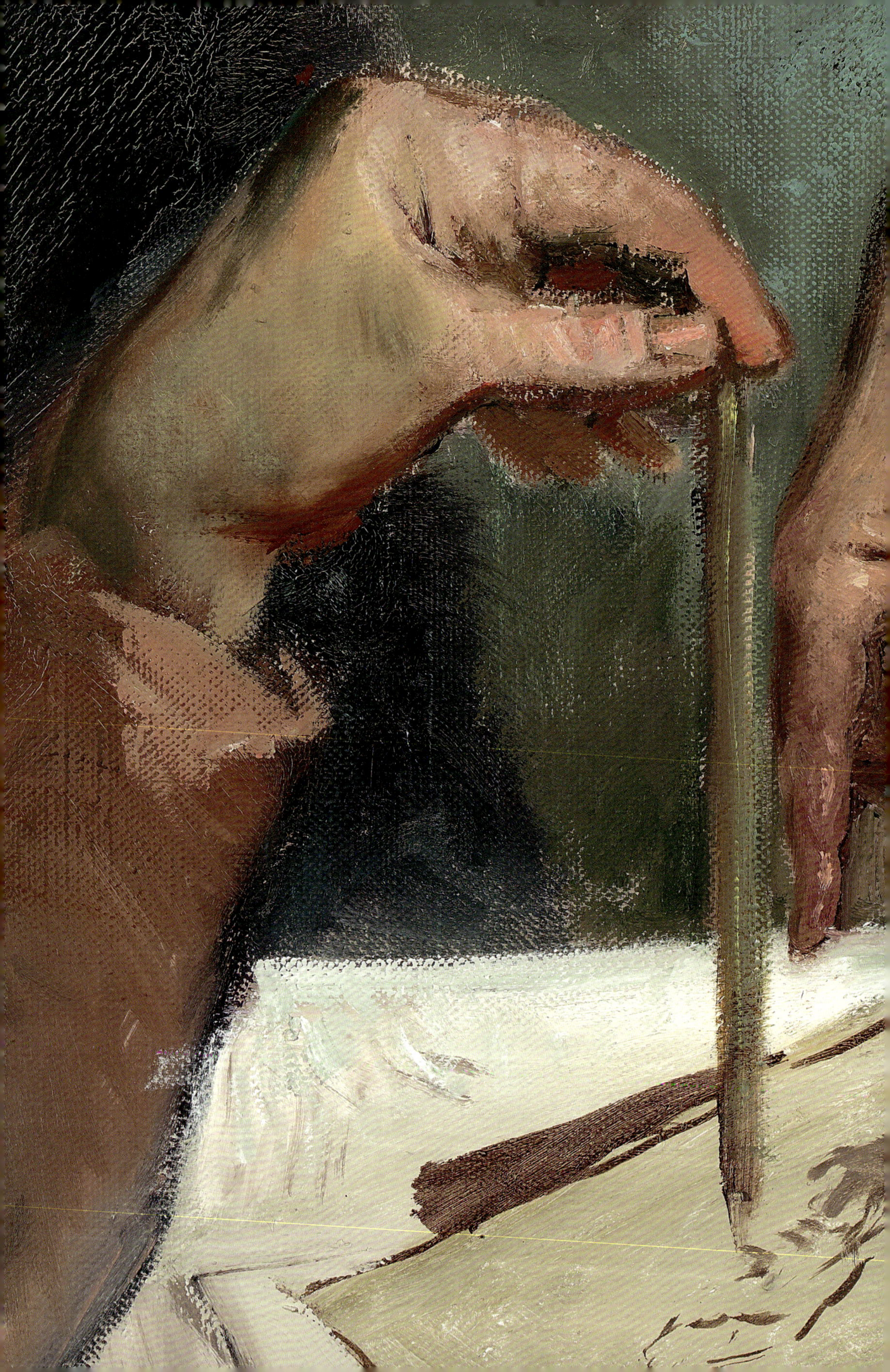

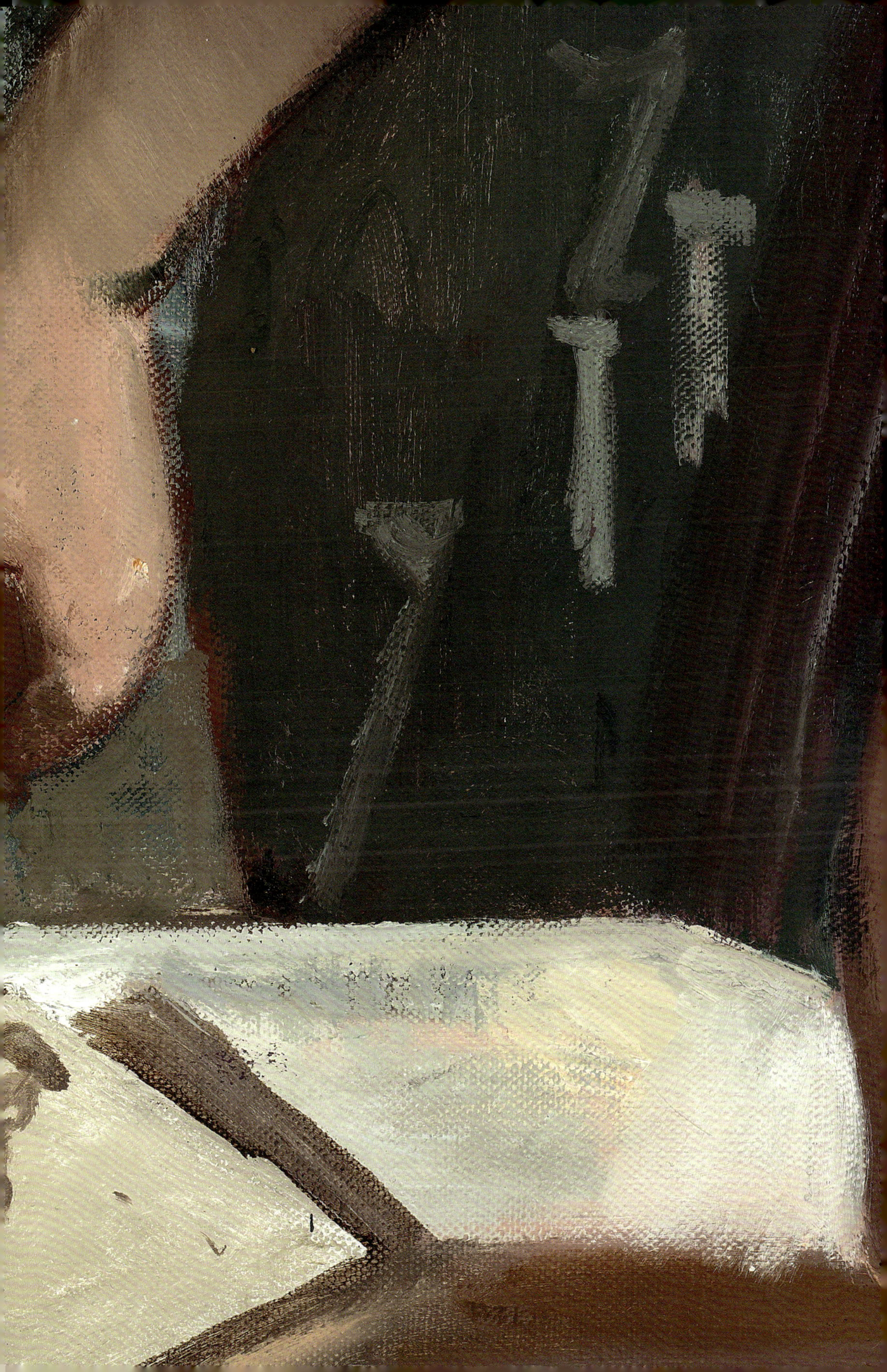

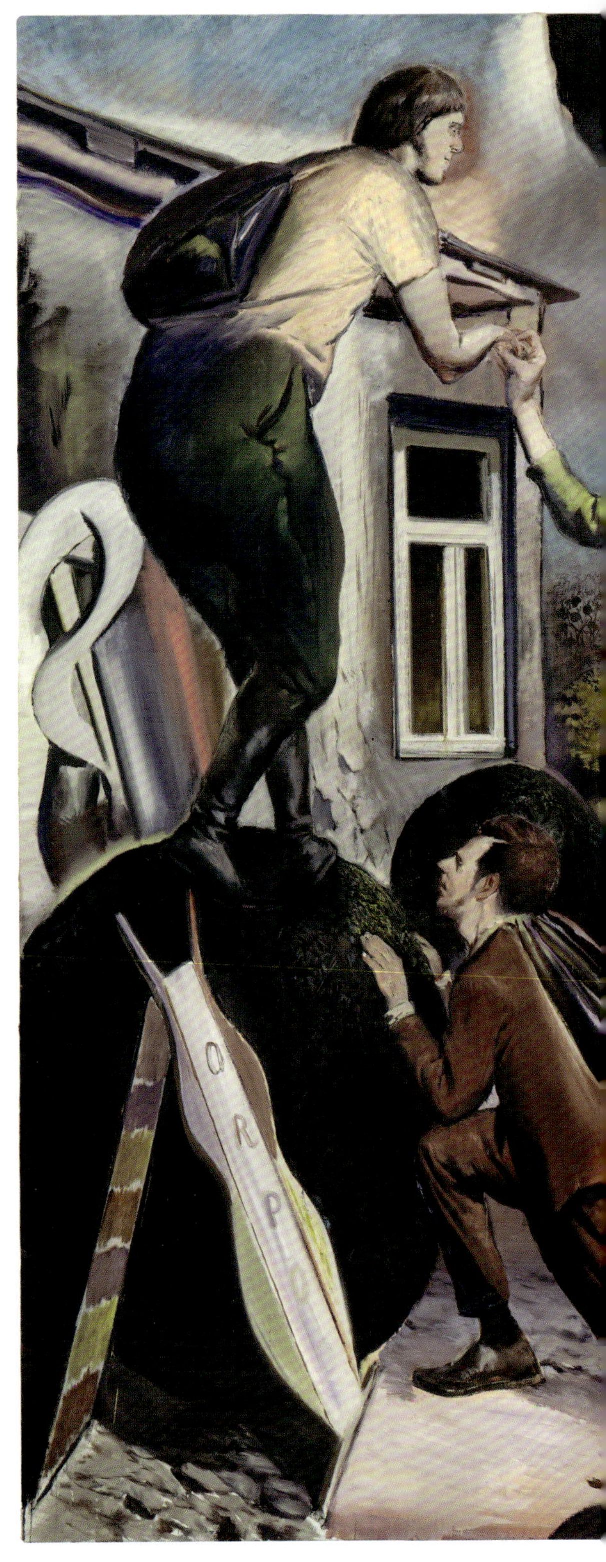

Käfer, 2017

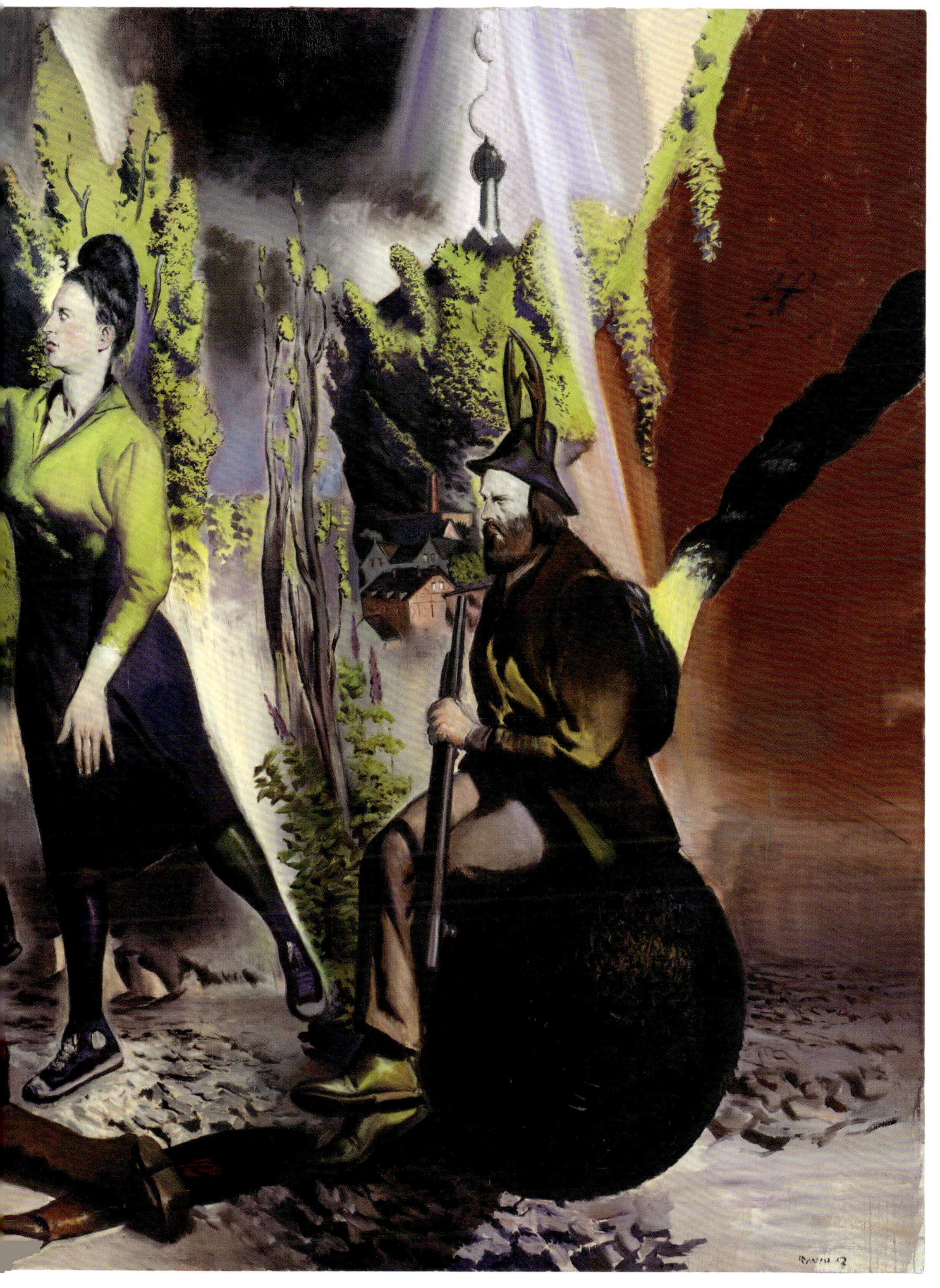

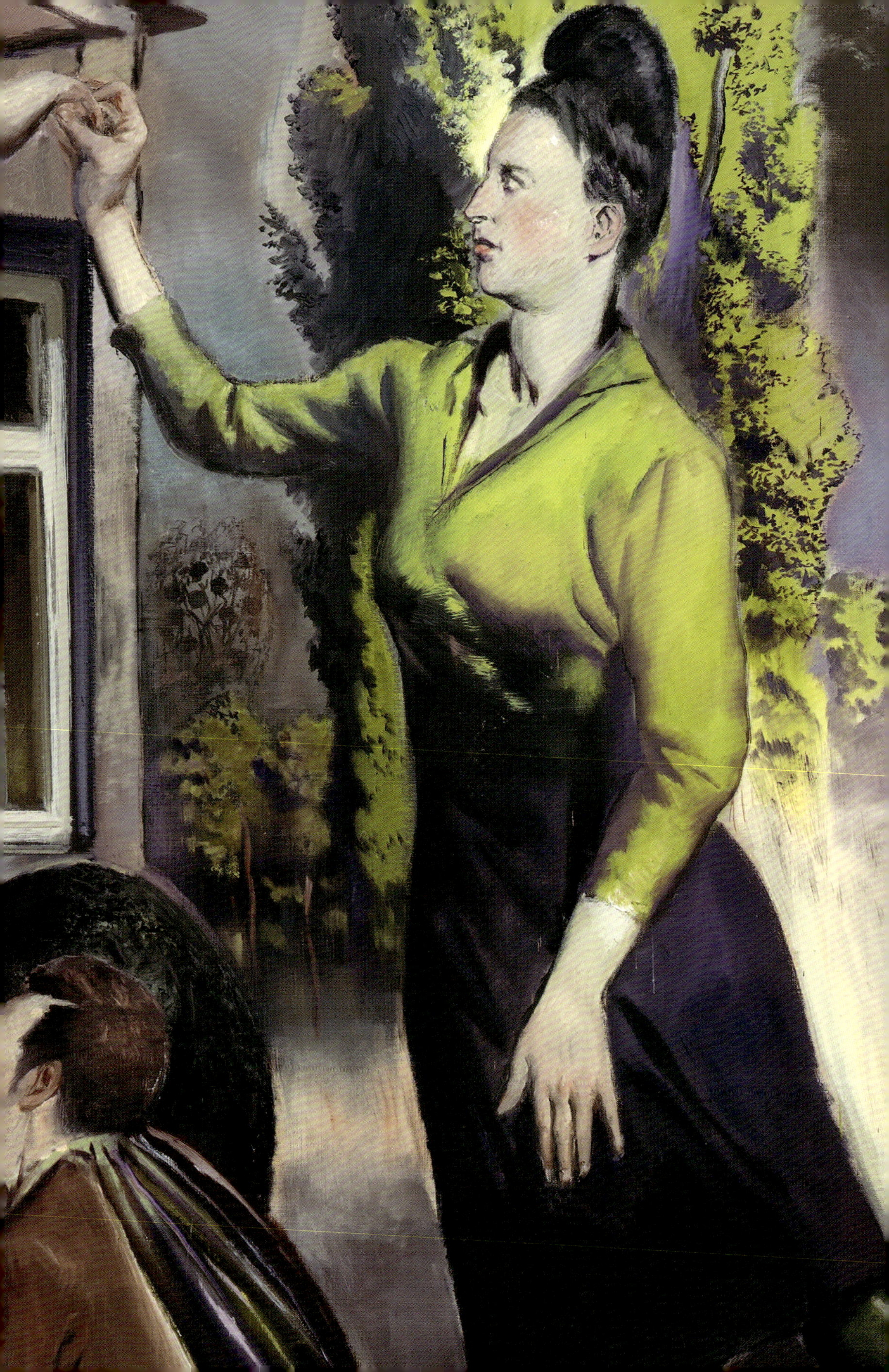

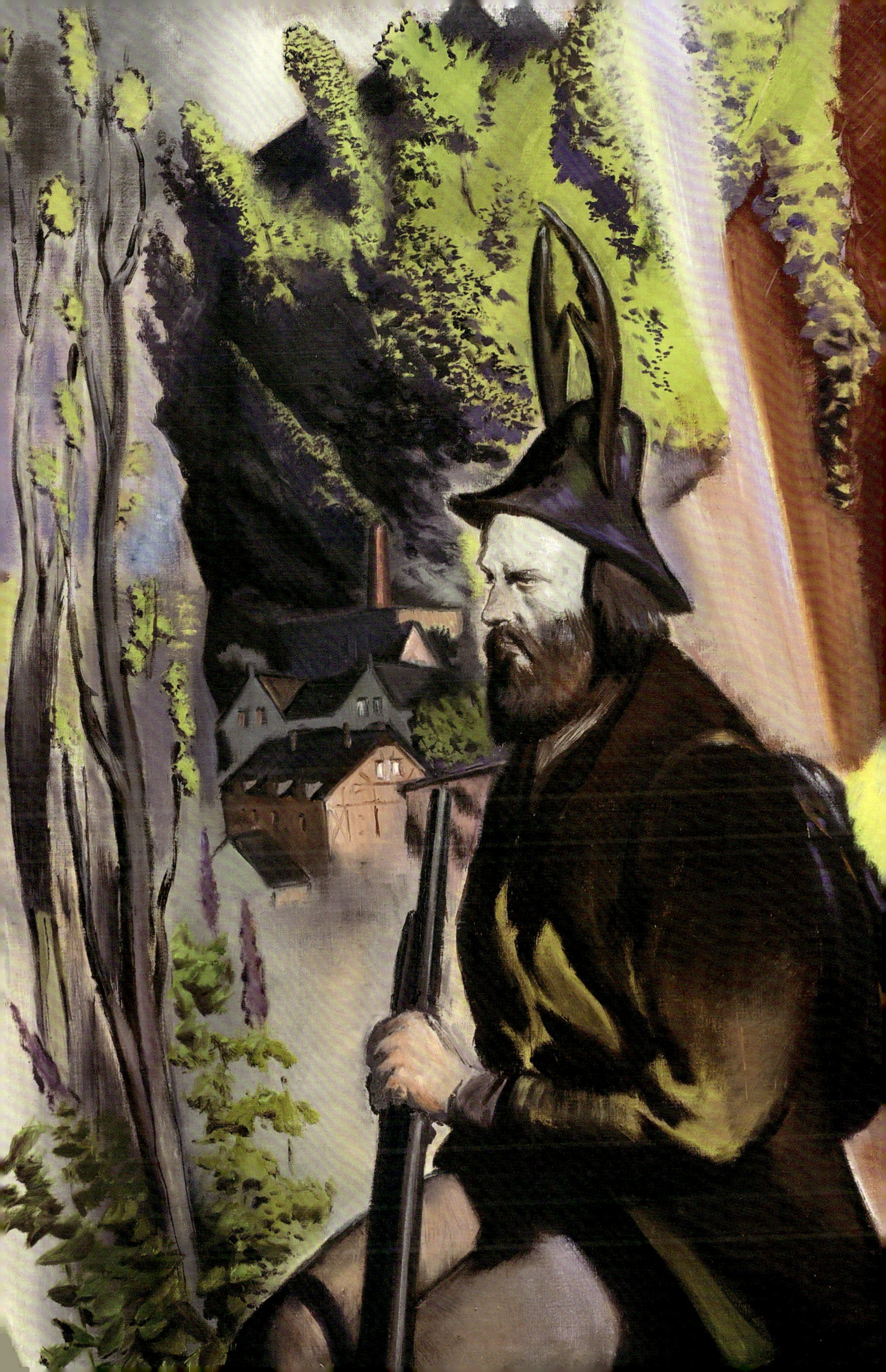

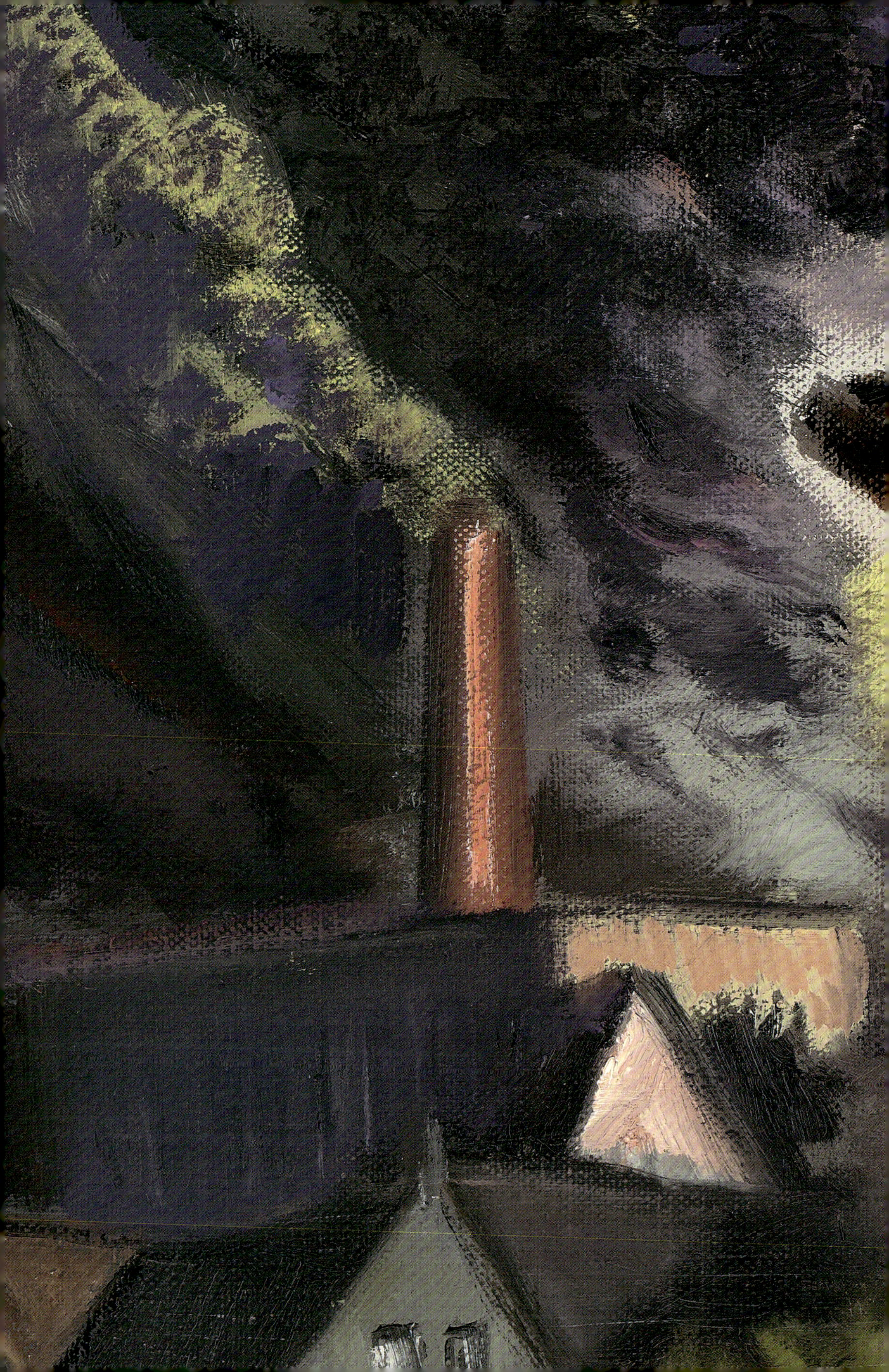

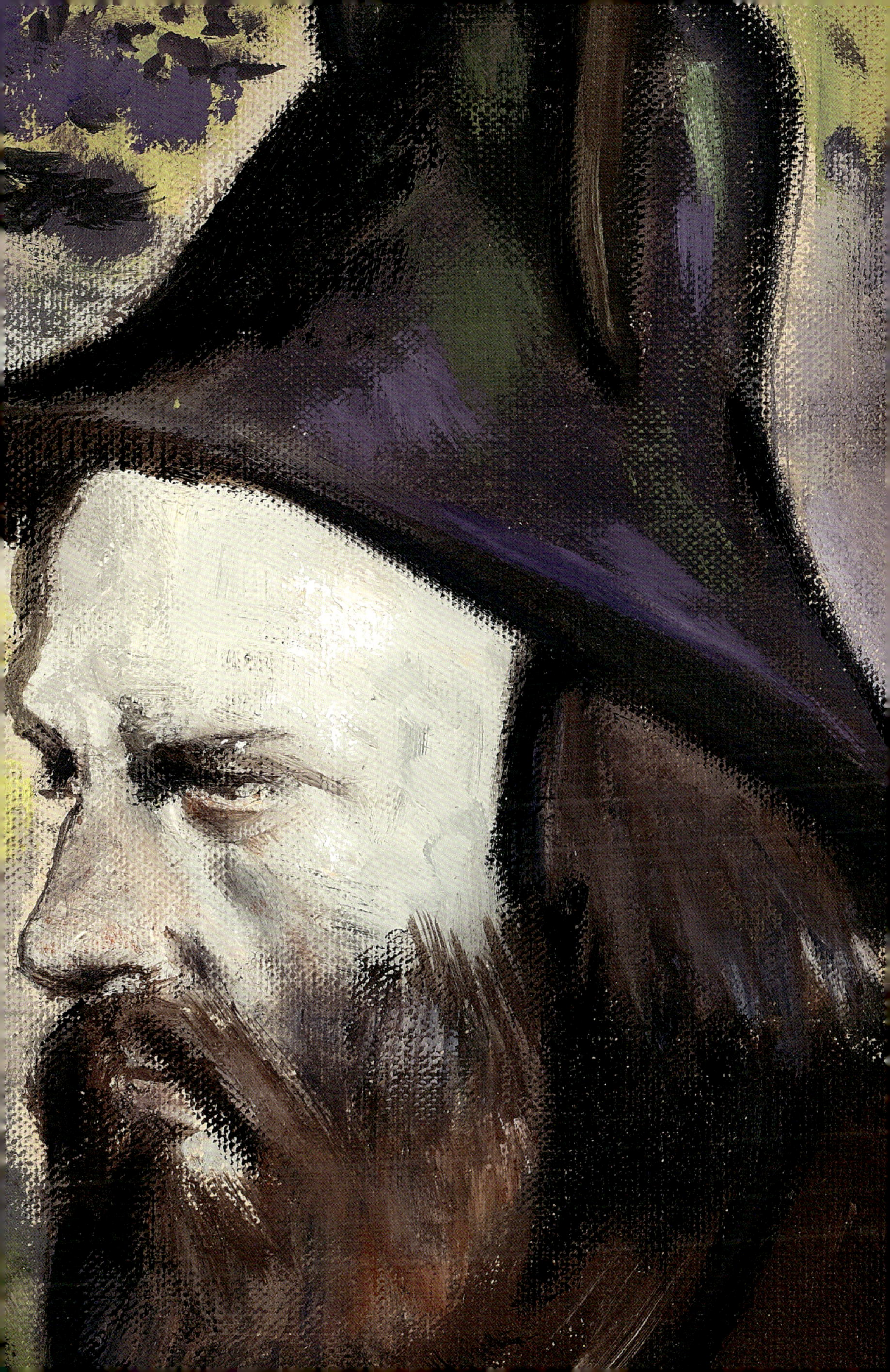

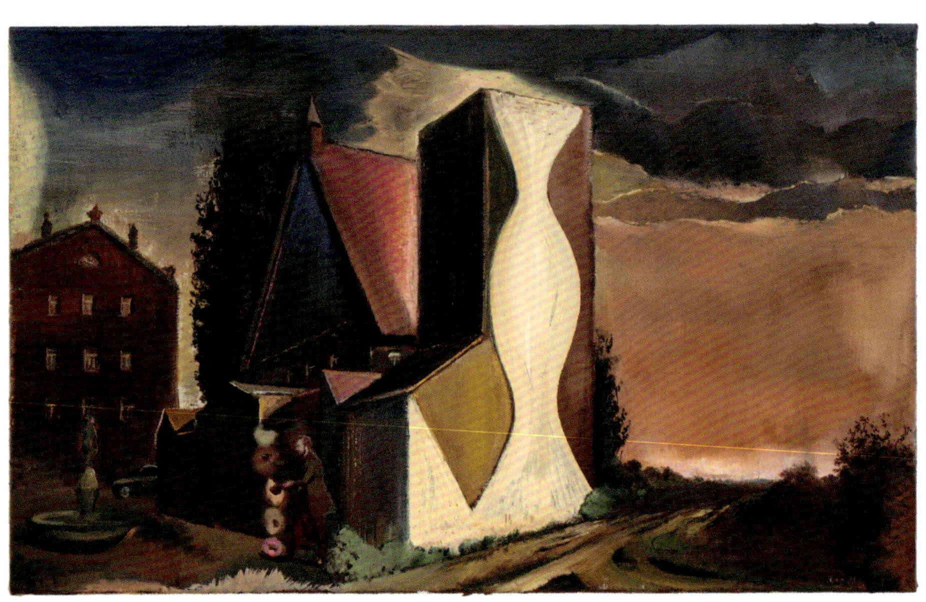

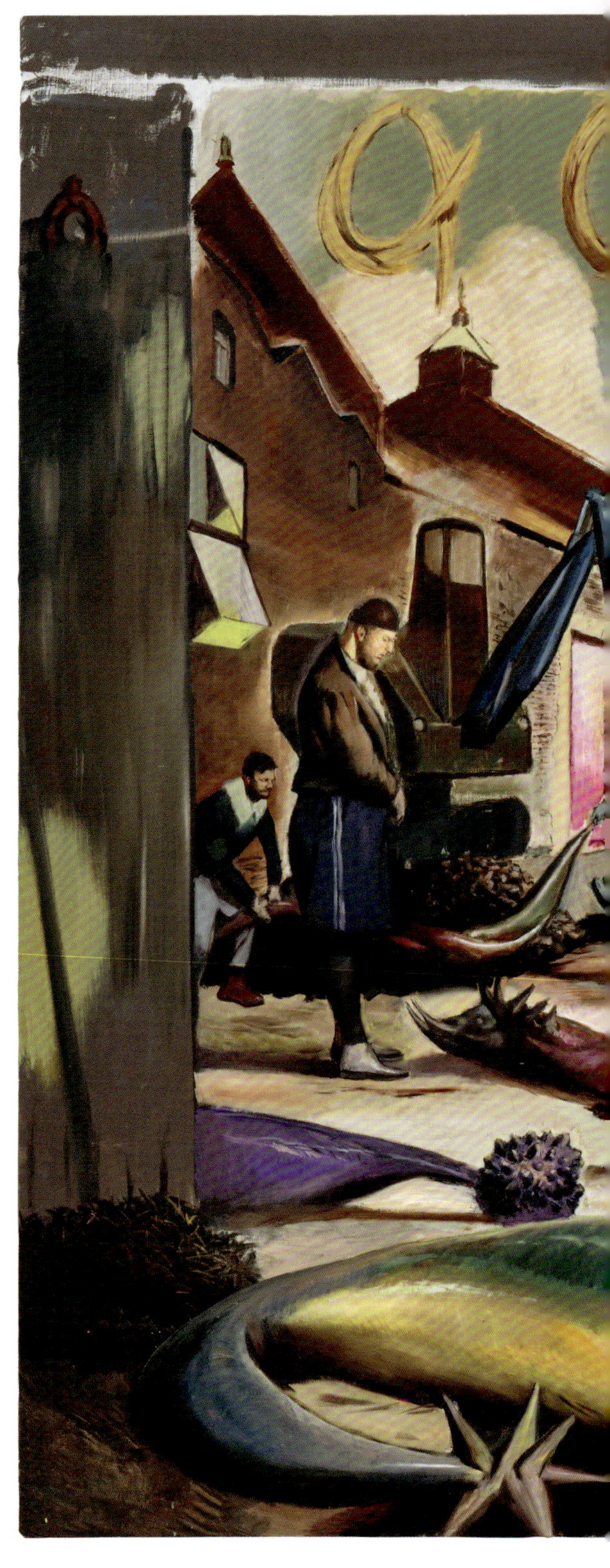

Propaganda, 2018

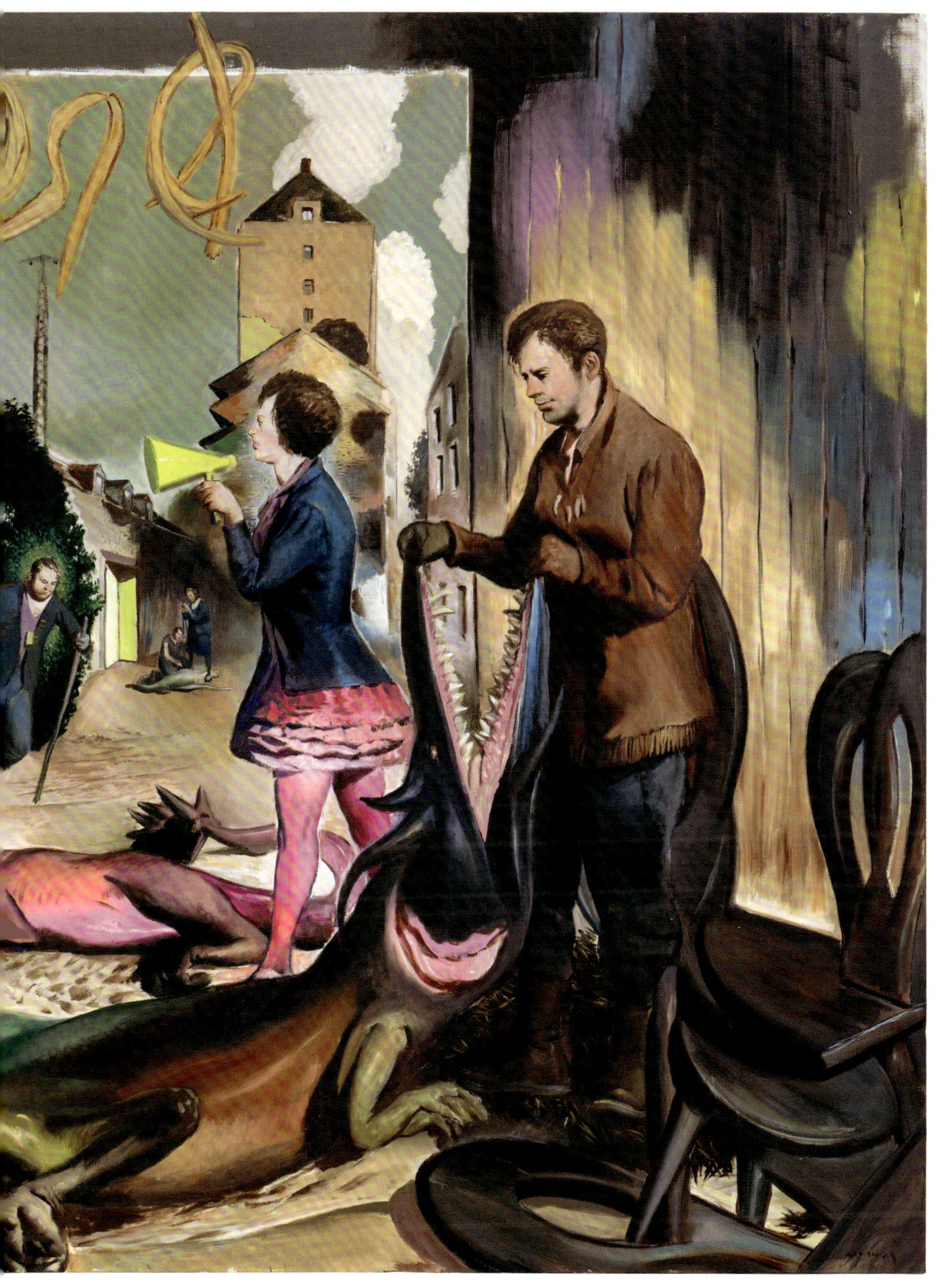

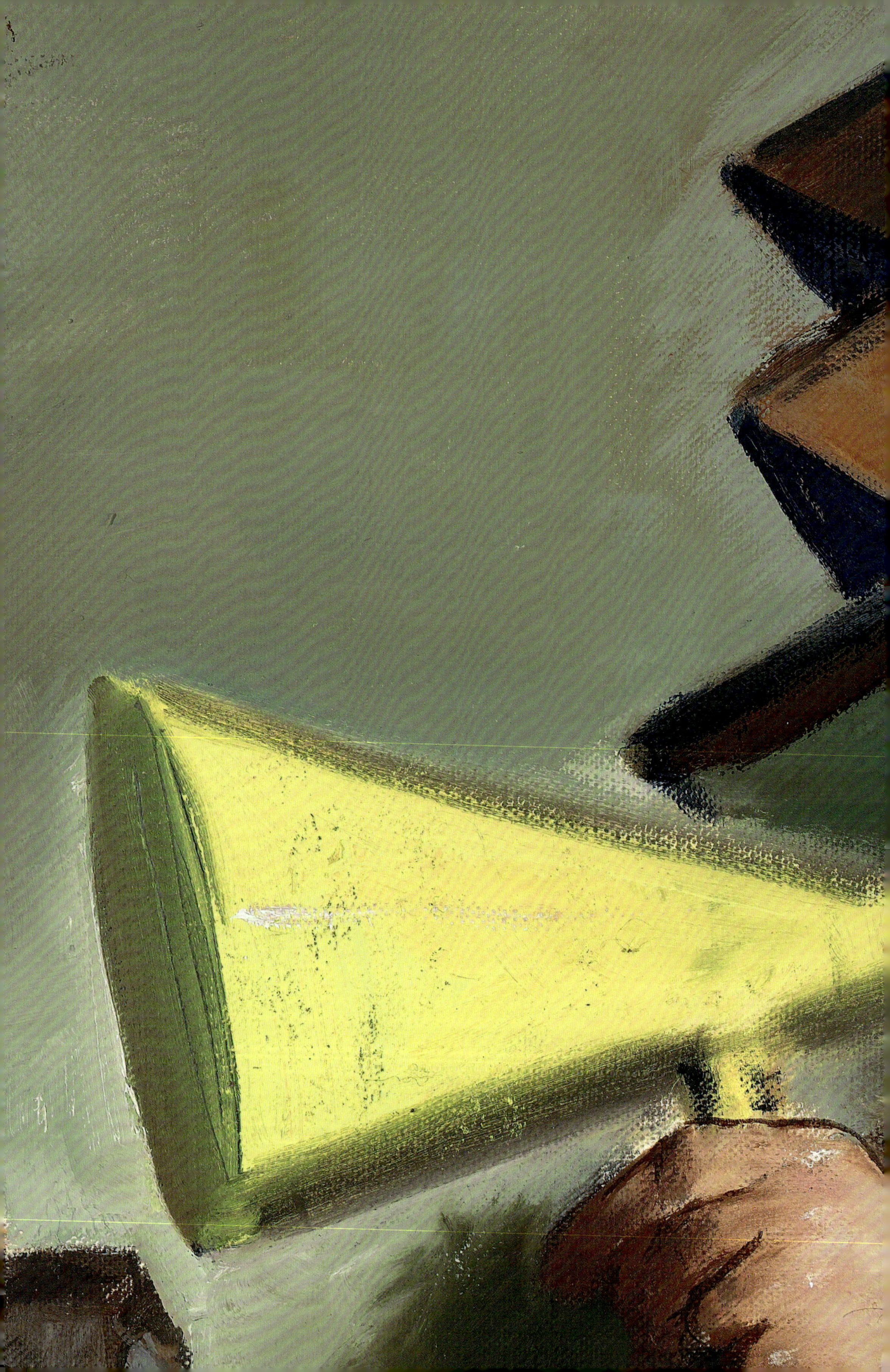

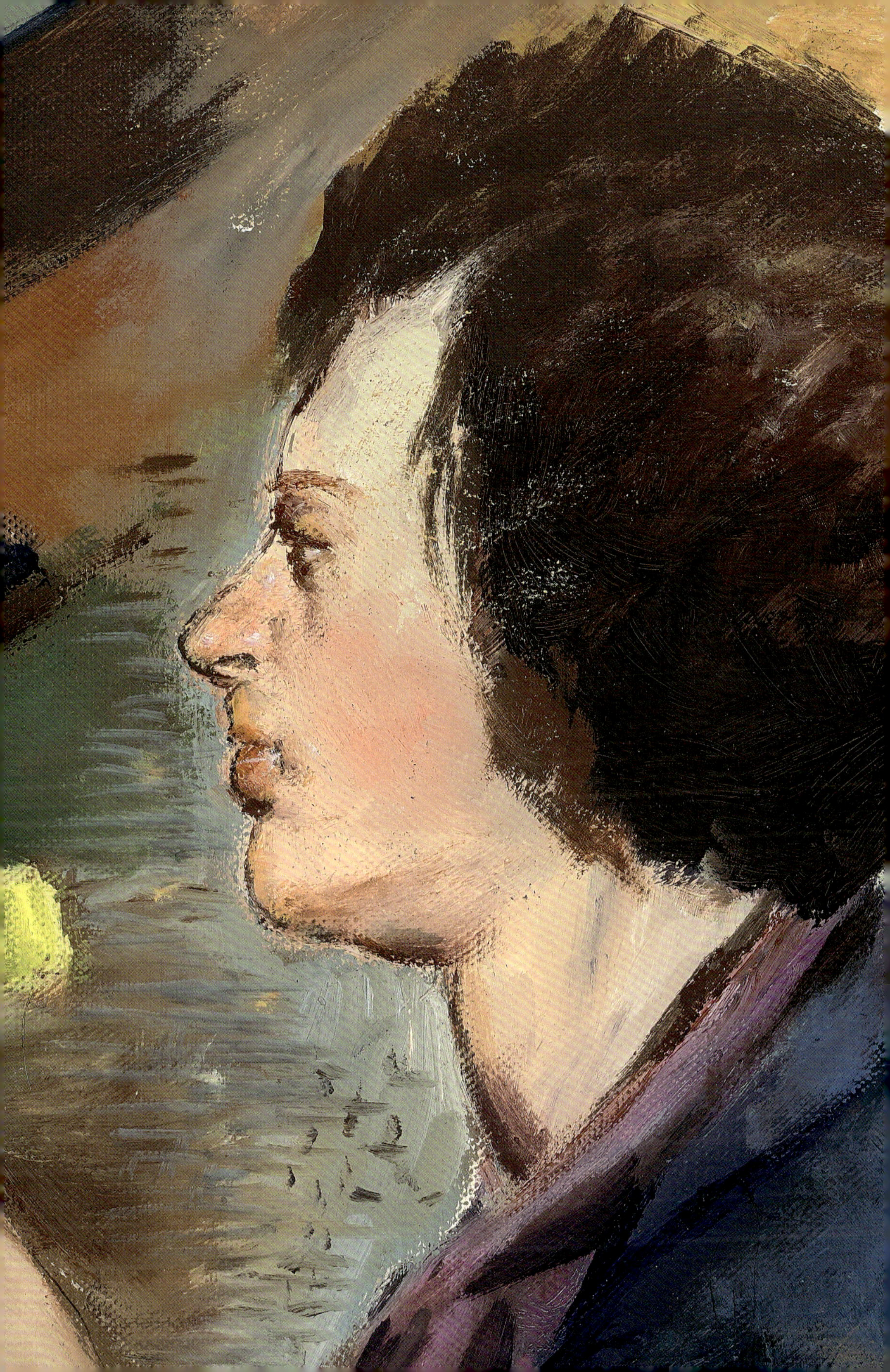

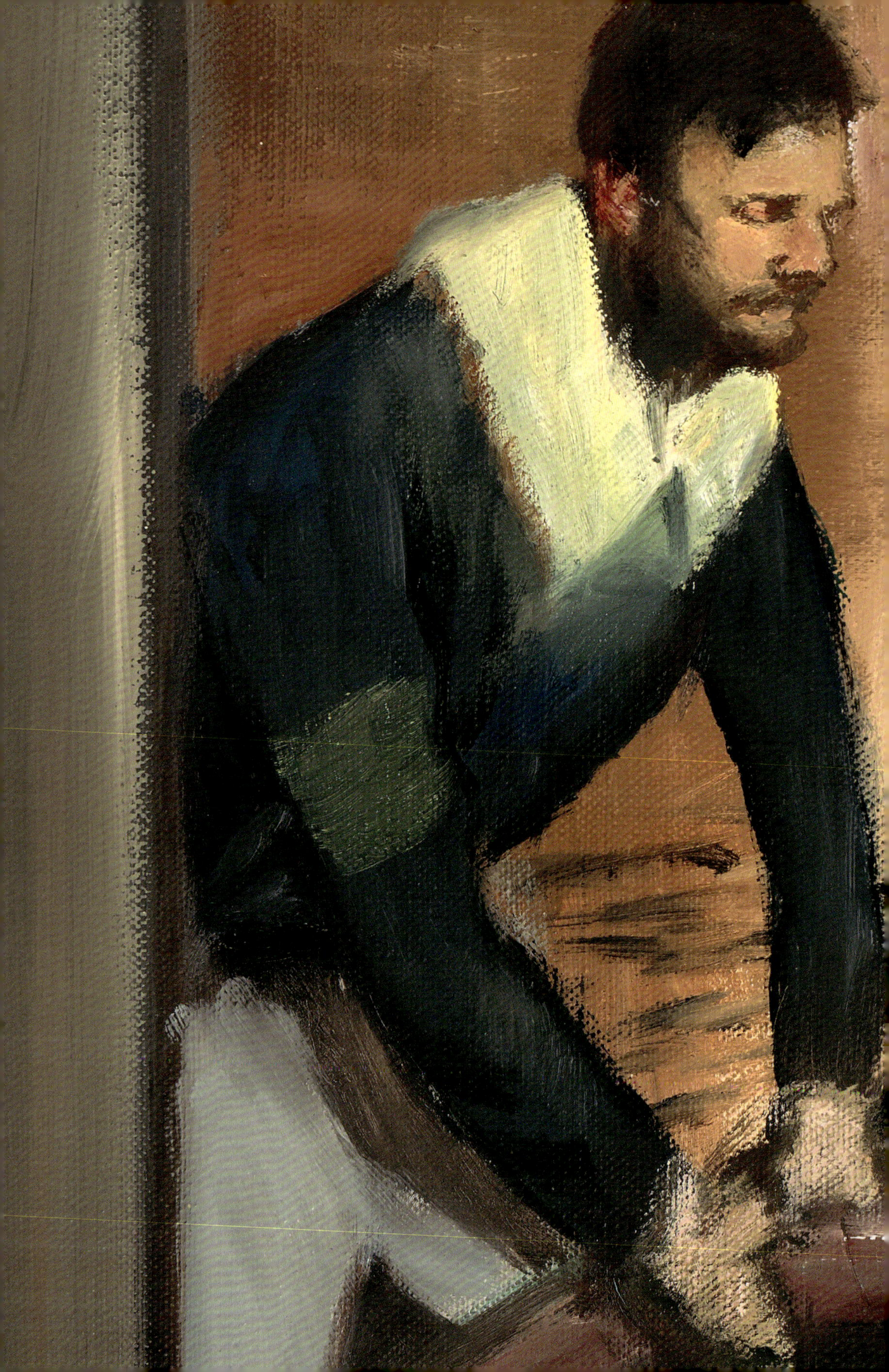

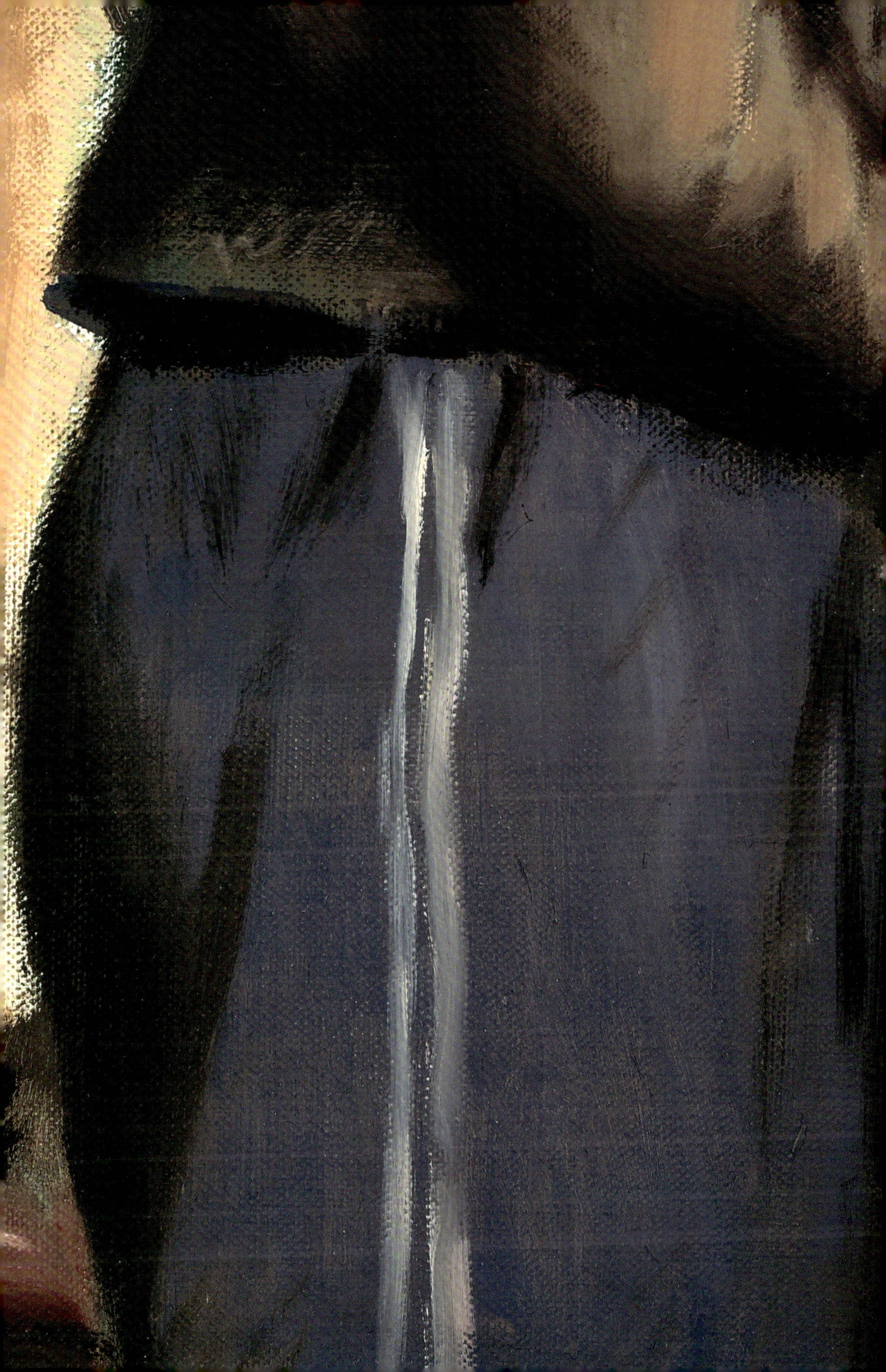

Brauner Bagger, 2018

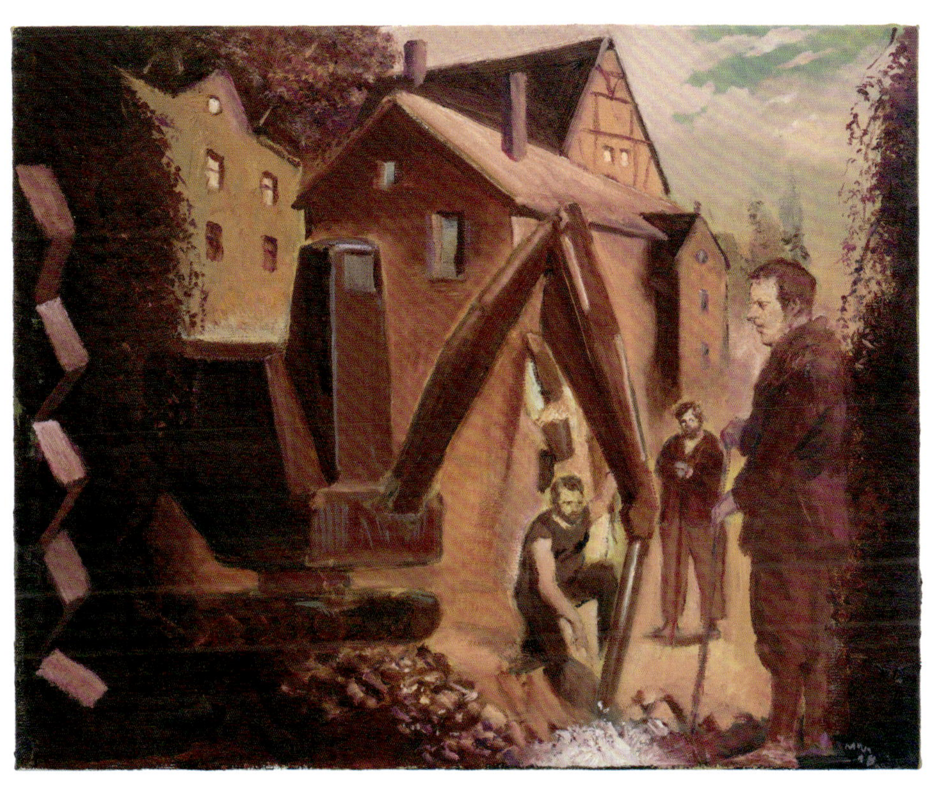

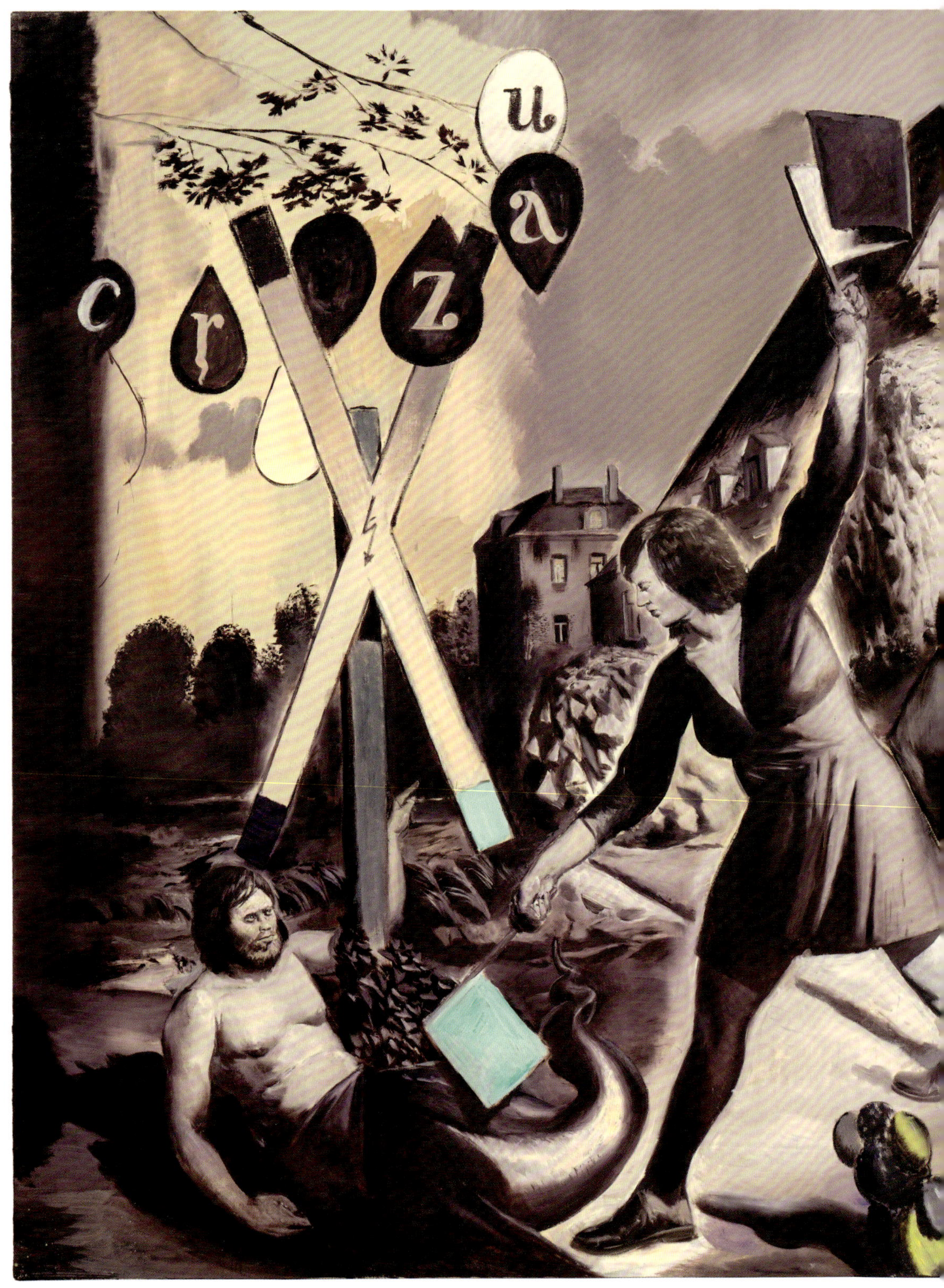
c
r
u
z
a

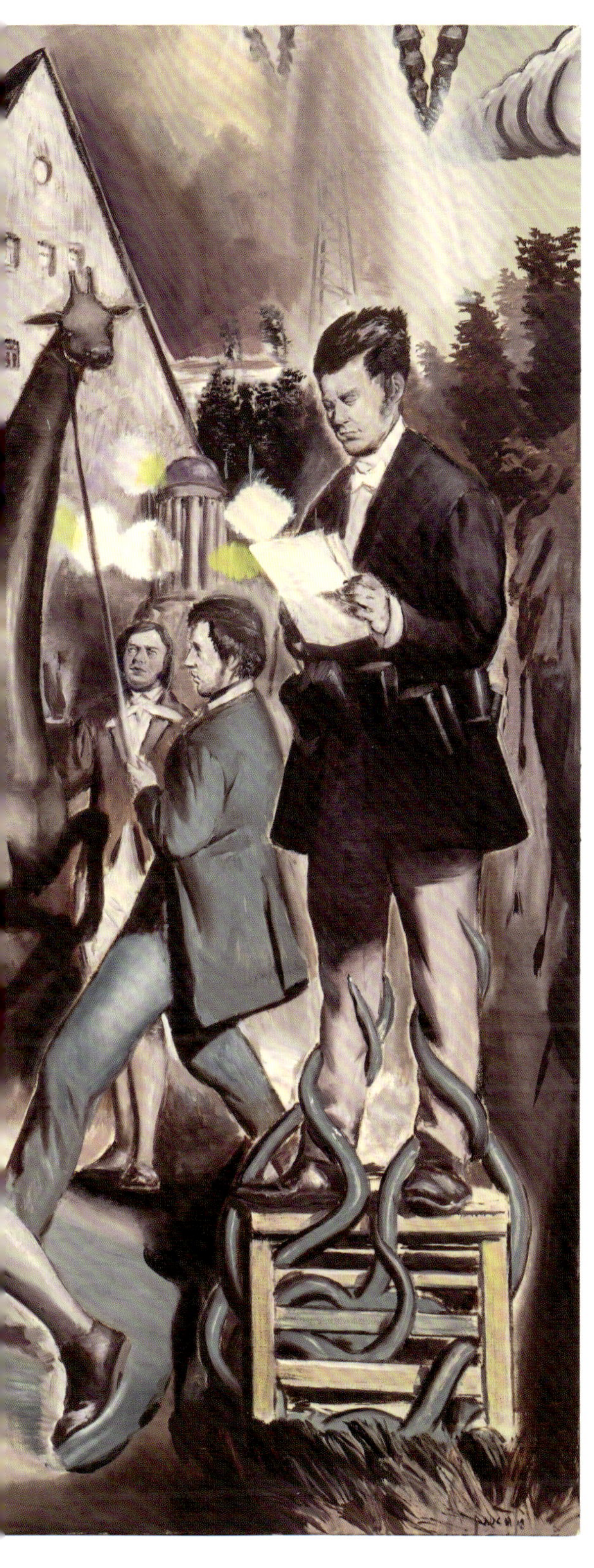

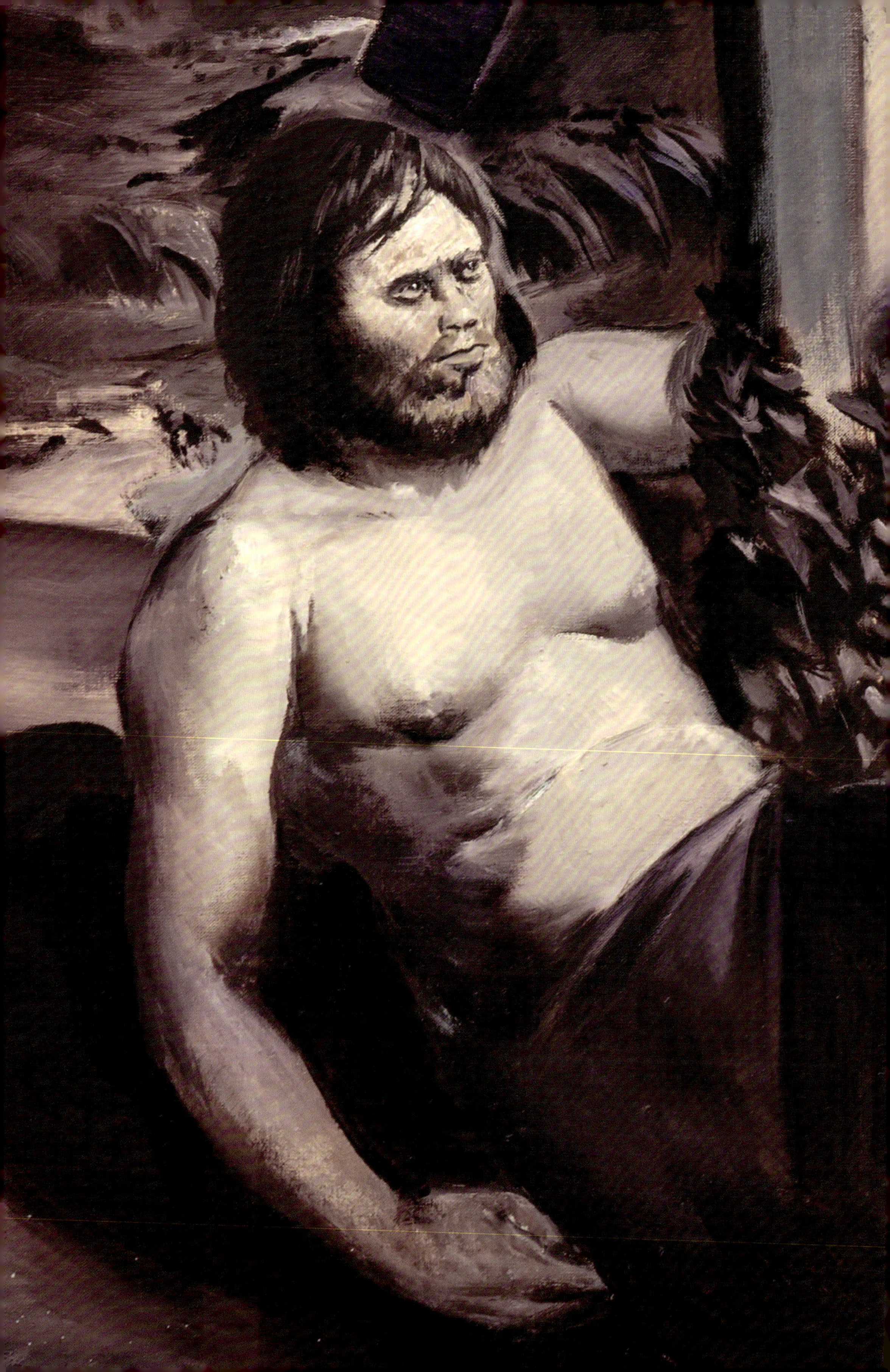

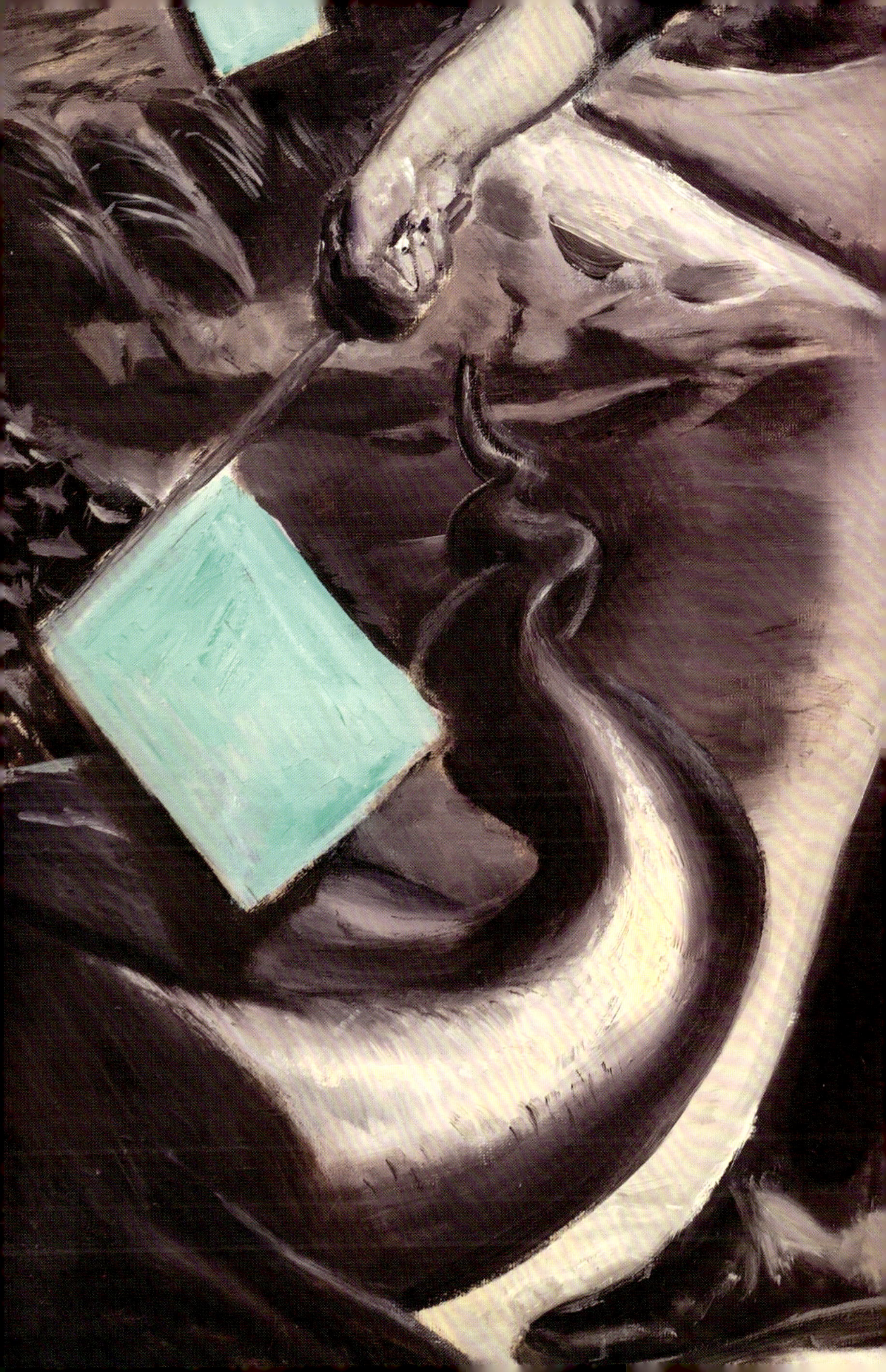

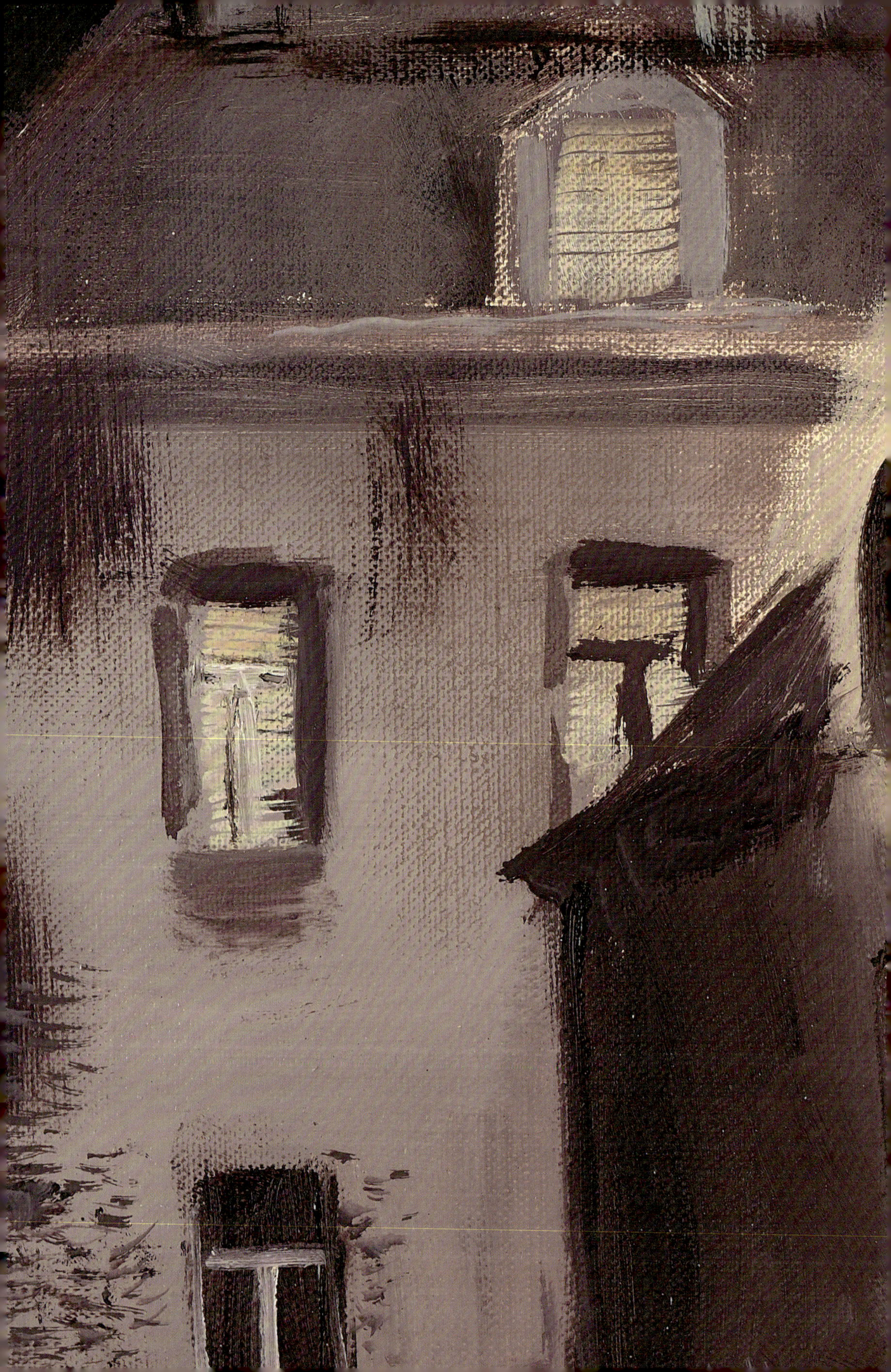

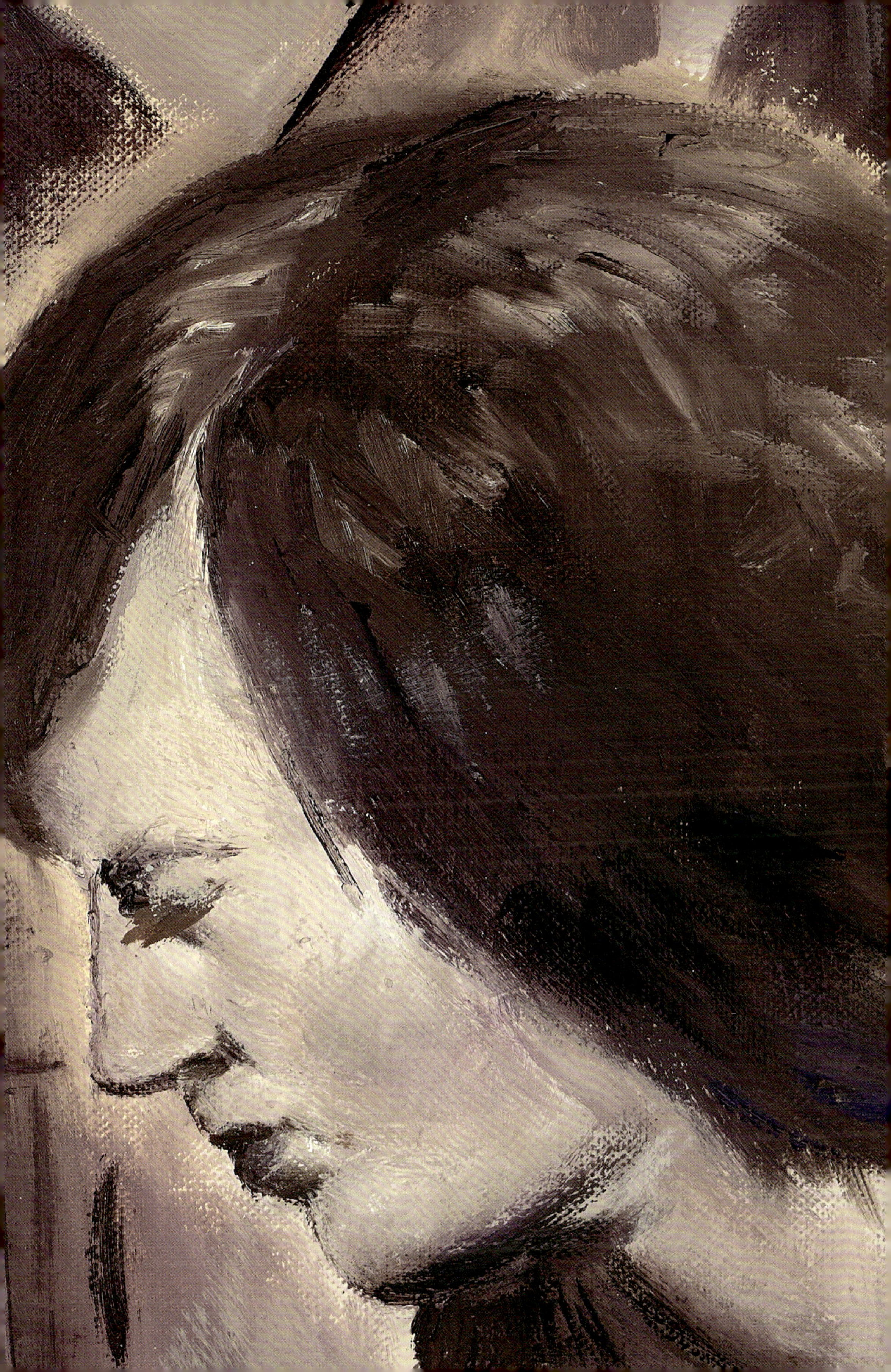

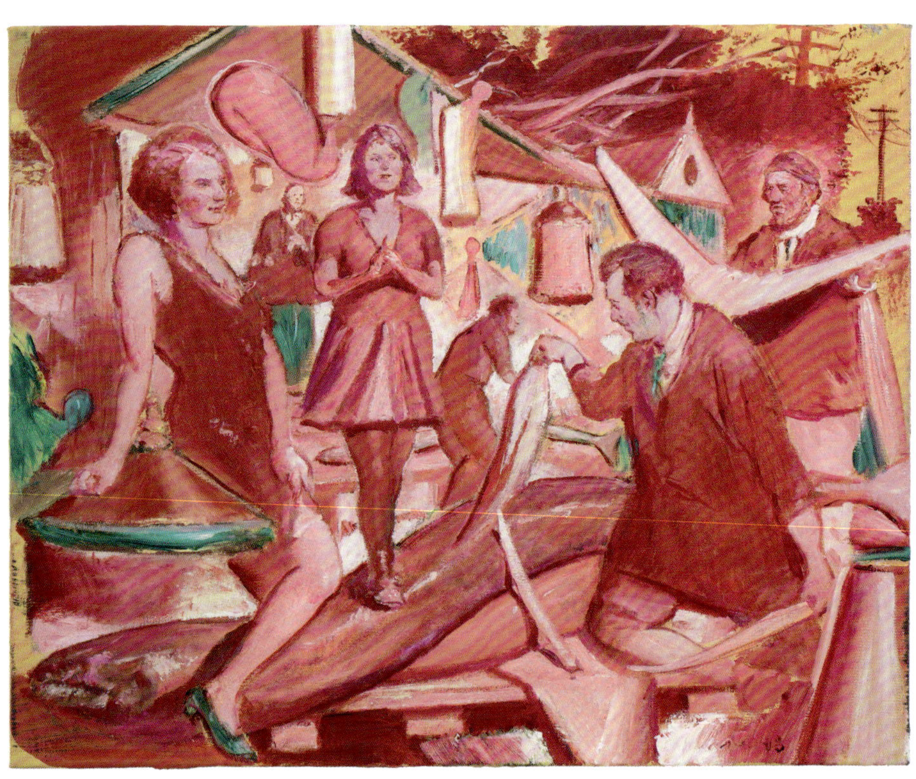

Luz, 2018

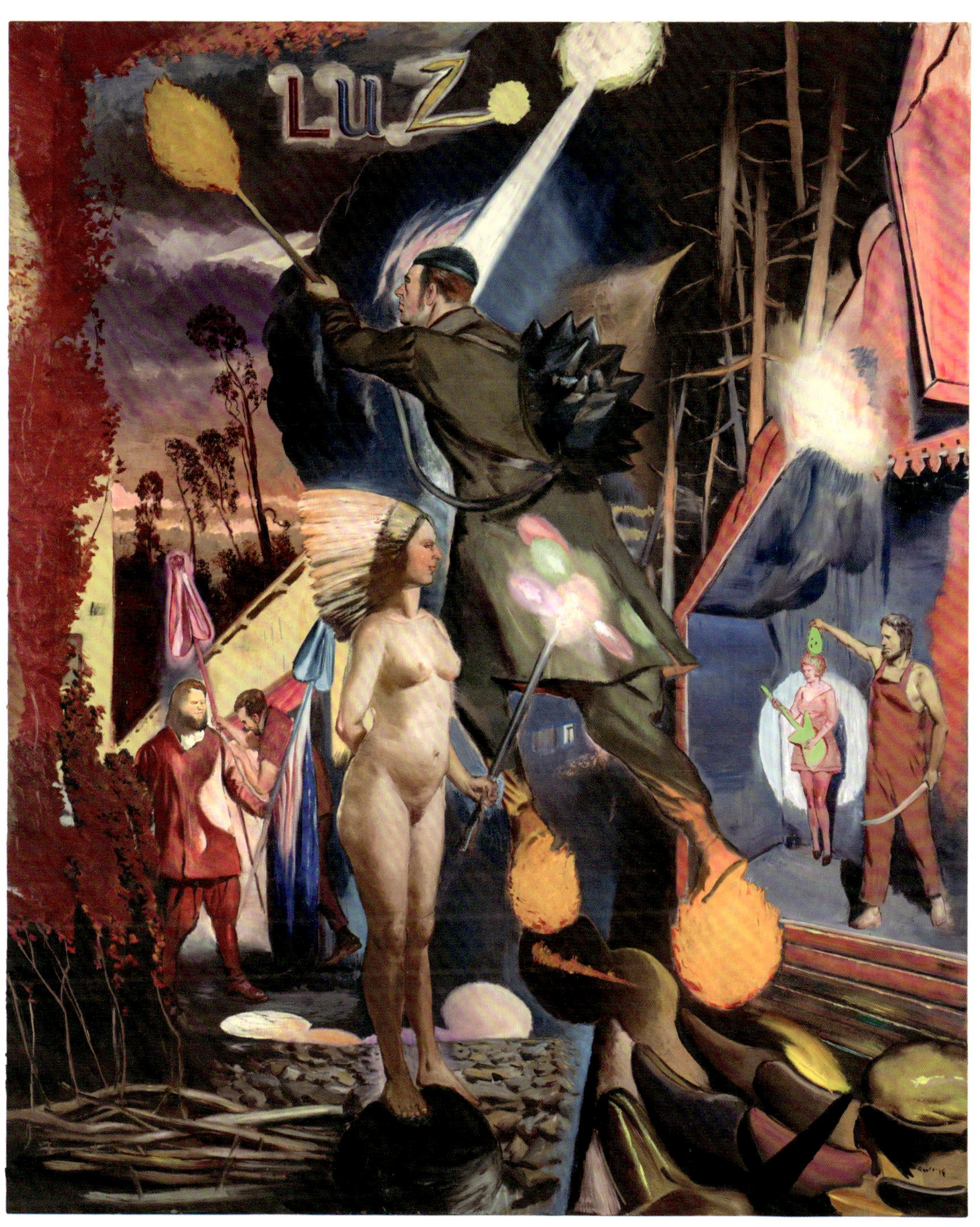
LuZ

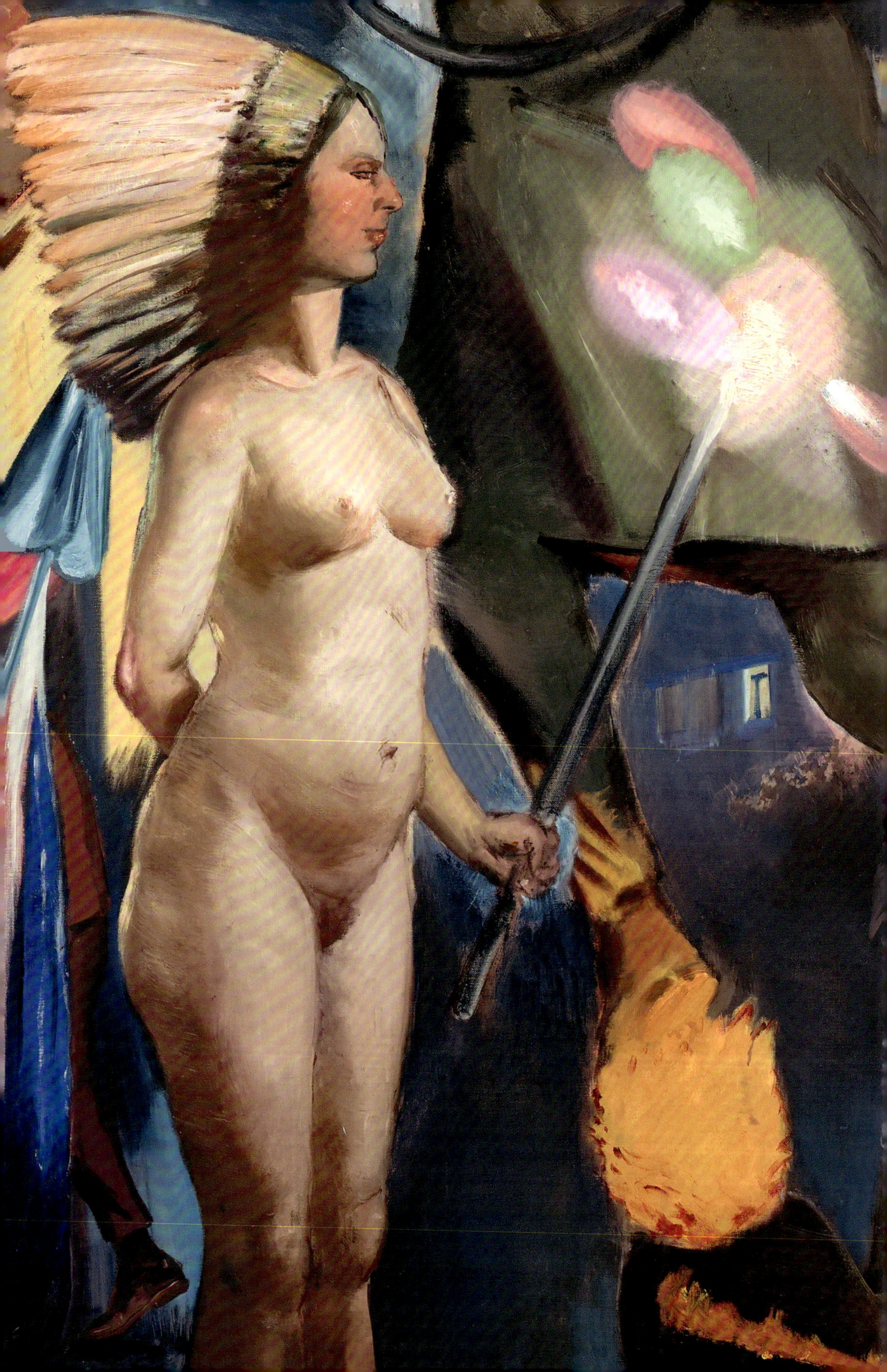

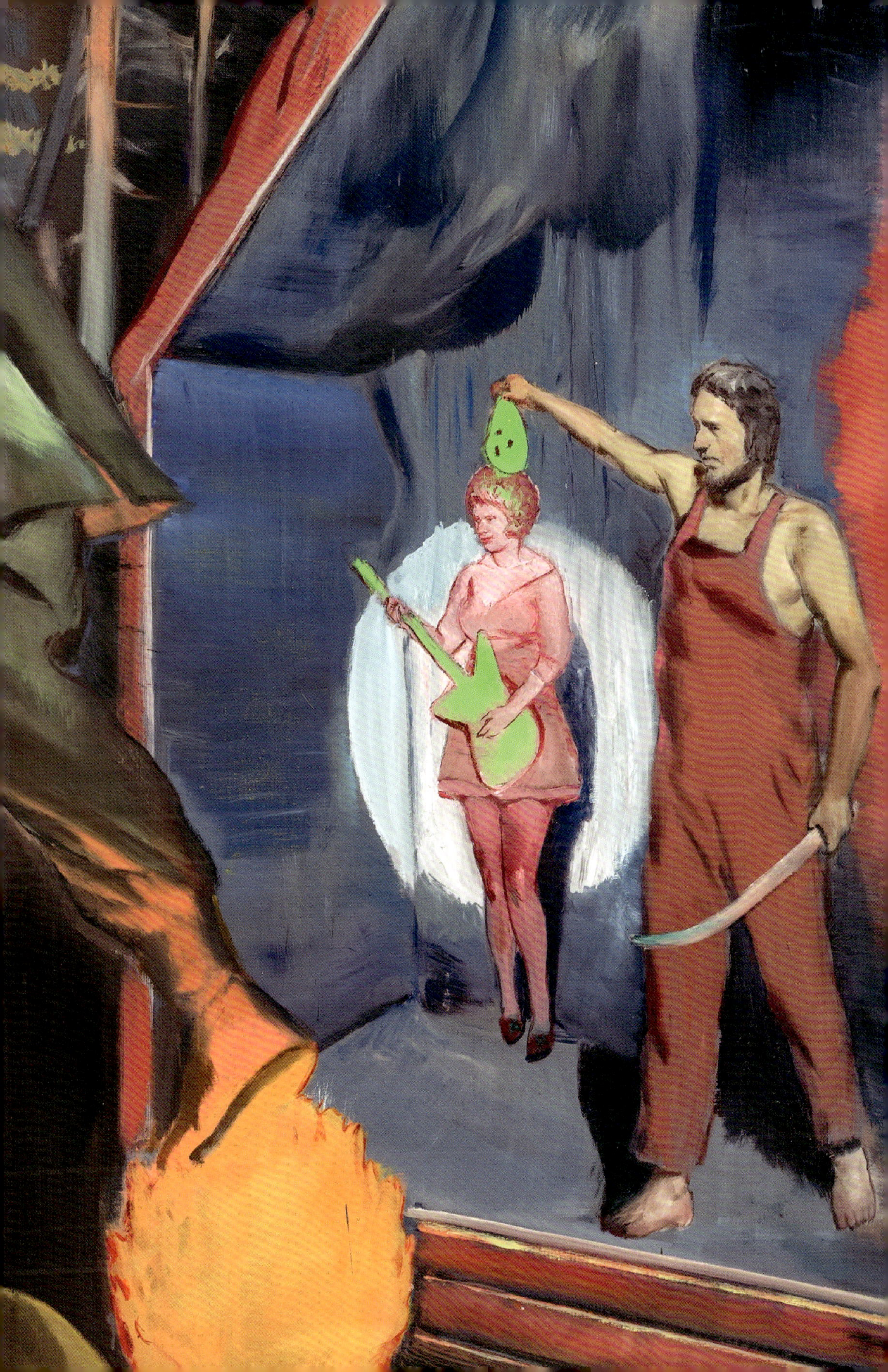

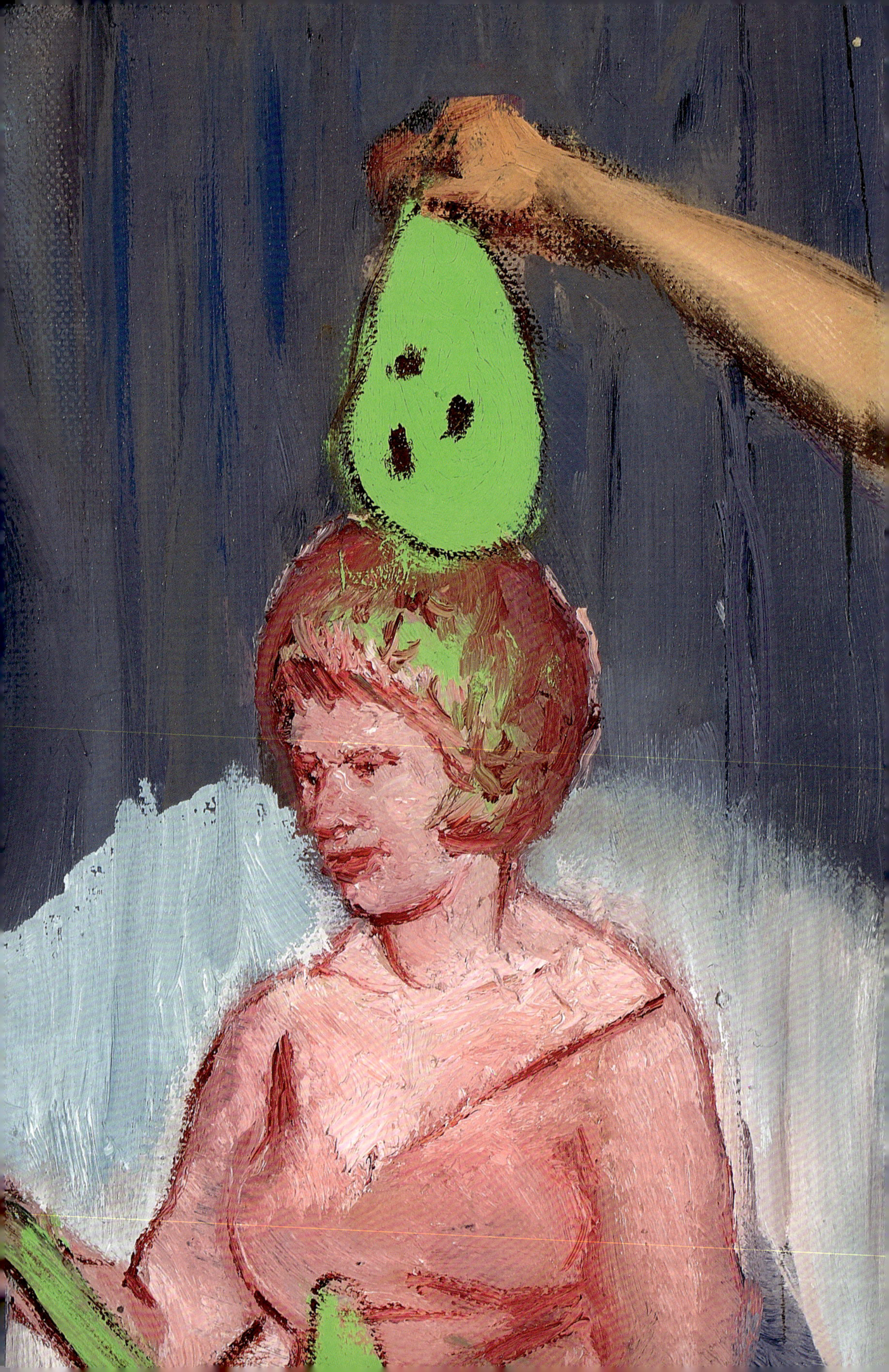

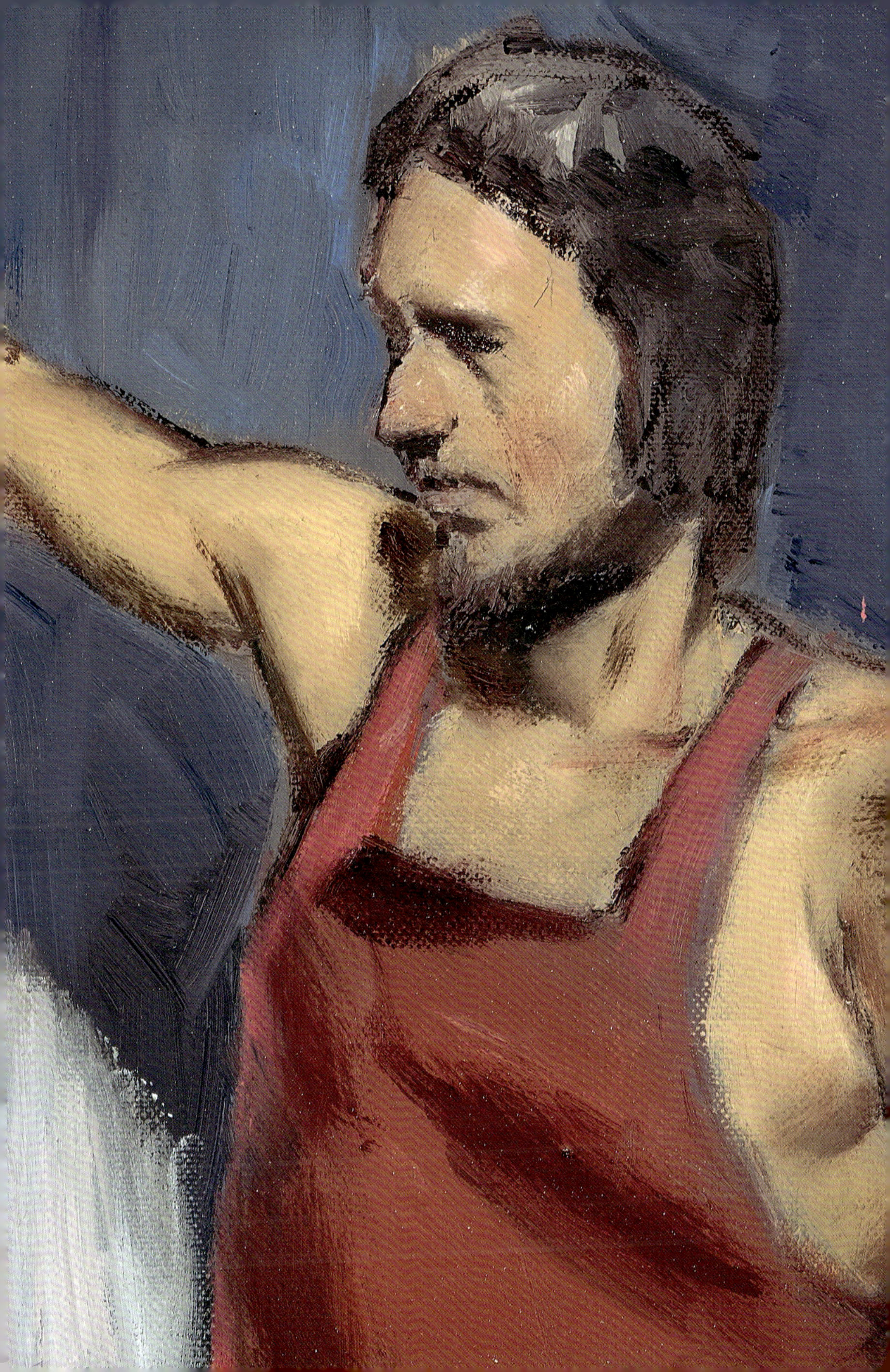

Tara, 2018
Oil on canvas
118 ⅛ × 98 ⅜ inches
300 × 250 cm
Pages 5, 6–7, 8–9

Anfahrt, 2018
Oil on canvas
9 ⅞ × 11 ¾ inches
25 × 30 cm
Page 10

Zahler, 2018
Oil on canvas
19 ⅝ × 15 ¾ inches
50 × 40 cm
Page 13

Kap, 2018
Oil on canvas
118 ⅛ × 98 ⅜ inches
300 × 250 cm
Pages 15, 16–17, 18–19

Sog, 2018
Oil on canvas
15 ¾ × 19 ⅝ inches
40 × 50 cm
Page 20

Der Wächter, 2018
Oil on canvas
19 ⅝ × 15 ¾ inches
50 × 40 cm
Page 23

Die Herrin, 2018
Oil on canvas
98 ⅜ × 118 ⅛ inches
250 × 300 cm
Pages 24–25, 26–27,
28–29

Zweifel, 2018
Oil on canvas
98 ⅜ × 118 ⅛ inches
250 × 300 cm
Pages 38–39, 40–41,
42–43

Käfer, 2017
Oil on canvas
98 ⅜ × 118 ⅛ inches
250 × 300 cm
Pages 44–45, 46–47,
48–49

Töpferhof, 2018
Oil on canvas
19 ⅝ × 33 ½ inches
50 × 85 cm
Page 50

Propaganda, 2018
Oil on canvas
98 ⅜ × 118 ⅛ inches
250 × 300 cm
Pages 52–53, 54–55,
56–57

Brauner Bagger, 2018
Oil on canvas
15 ¾ × 19 ⅝ inches
40 × 50 cm
Page 59

Sperre, 2018
Oil on canvas
98 ⅜ × 118 ⅛ inches
250 × 300 cm
Pages 60–61, 62–63,
64–65

Der Aufschneider, 2018
Oil on canvas
15 ¾ × 19 ⅝ inches
40 × 50 cm
Page 66

Luz, 2018
Oil on canvas
118 ⅛ × 98 ⅜ inches
300 × 250 cm
Pages 69, 70–71,
72–73

Neo Rauch was born in 1960 in Leipzig, Germany, where he currently lives and works. He studied at the Hochschule für Grafik und Buchkunst, Leipzig, where he went on to teach. The artist's first solo museum presentation took place in 1997 at the Museum der bildenden Künste Leipzig. In 2010, his first major museum survey was co-hosted by the Museum der bildenden Künste Leipzig and the Pinakothek der Moderne, Munich. A version of this exhibition was shown at the Zachęta National Gallery of Art, Warsaw, in 2011.

Over the past decades, Rauch has had solo presentations at institutions including the Bonnefantenmuseum, Maastricht (2002); Centro de Arte Contemporáneo de Málaga, Spain (2005); Musée d'art contemporain de Montréal (2006); The Metropolitan Museum of Art, New York (2007); Museum Frieder Burda, Baden-Baden, Germany (2011); BOZAR – Centre for Fine Arts, Brussels (2013); and The Drawing Center, New York (2019).

The Grafikstiftung Neo Rauch, a foundation dedicated to maintaining and preserving Rauch's graphic oeuvre, opened in June 2012 in the artist's hometown of Aschersleben, Germany.

Museum collections that hold works by the artist include Hamburger Bahnhof – Museum für Gegenwart, Berlin; The Metropolitan Museum of Art, New York; Museum der bildenden Künste Leipzig; The Museum of Modern Art, New York; Pinakothek der Moderne, Munich; Solomon R. Guggenheim Museum, New York; and the Stedelijk Museum, Amsterdam.

Daniel Kehlmann was born in Munich in 1975 and lives in Berlin and New York. His literary works have won the Candide Prize, Doderer Prize, Kleist Prize, Thomas Mann Prize, and the Welt Literature Prize. His novel *Measuring the World* (2007) has been translated into forty languages, including Chinese.

Published by David Zwirner
Books on the occasion of

Neo Rauch: PROPAGANDA
David Zwirner
5–6/F, H Queen's
80 Queen's Road Central
Central, Hong Kong
March 26–May 4, 2019

David Zwirner Books
529 West 20th Street
2nd Floor
New York, New York 10011
+1 212 727 2070
davidzwirnerbooks.com

Managing Director:
Doro Globus
Editorial Director:
Lucas Zwirner

Project Editor:
Elizabeth Gordon
Production Assistant:
Elizabeth Koehler
Photography Coordinator:
Rebecca Ashby-Colón
Proofreader:
Anna Drozda

Design: Chris Wu and
Ella Viscardi, Wkshps
Production Manager:
Paul Au, Gray Balance
Studio Limited
Color Separations:
Paul Au, Gray Balance
Studio Limited
Printing: Asia One,
Hong Kong

Typeface: Styrene B
Paper: Kinmari Matt EX,
157 gsm

Publication © 2019
David Zwirner Books
"Becoming Caligari:
A Fantasy Inspired by
Neo Rauch's Art"
© 2019 Daniel Kehlmann.
Translation from
the German © 2019
Ross Benjamin

All artwork © 2019
Neo Rauch

All photography by
Uwe Walter

Distributed in the United
States and Canada by
Simon & Schuster, Inc.
1230 Avenue of the Americas
New York, New York 10020
simonandschuster.com

Distributed outside the
United States and Canada
by Thames & Hudson, Ltd.
181A High Holborn
London WC1V 7QX
thamesandhudson.com

ISBN 978-1-64423-011-4
Library of Congress Control
Number: 2019931546

Printed in Hong Kong

Cover: *Die Herrin*, 2018
(detail)

Acknowledgments

David Zwirner wishes to
thank Neo Rauch, without
whom this exhibition and
catalogue would not have
been possible, as well as
Rosa Loy and Hanna
Schouwink. We are especially
grateful to Daniel Kehlmann
for his insightful text.
Thank you also to Rebecca
Ashby-Colón, Paul Au,
Ross Benjamin, Nadia Chan,
Angela Choon, Yan Chuan,
Anna Drozda, Francesca
Frediani, Doro Globus,
Elizabeth Gordon, McClain
Groff, Qianfan Gu, Will Hine,
Tony Huang, Claudia Ip,
Isabel Jiang, Guo Juan,
Fouad Kanaan, Hope Kang,
Elizabeth Koehler, Joe Lam,
Charlotte Panis, Sylvia
Seufert, Dylan Shuai, Alec
Smyth, Molly Stein,
Ella Viscardi, Uwe Walter,
Ernest Wan, Anne Wehr,
Elaine Wong, Chris Wu,
Chris Xie, Leo Xu, Jeanine
Zhan, Lucas Zwirner, and
all the staff at David
Zwirner, New York, London,
and Hong Kong.